YOUR NAMING & DEFINING

Owning Your True Identity

Book # 1 From The "Seasoned For Destiny" Series

Sally Mahihu

Table of Contents

Chapter 1

IDENTIFIED FOR DESTINY

Understanding "The Who" You Were Born To Be and Embracing Your True Identity

Chapter 2

THE PASSWORDS TO YOUR TRUE IDENTITY

Knowing What Should and What Should Not Define You

Chapter 3

THE TRIGGERS TO AN IDENTITY CRISIS

Arresting Your Identity Thieves

Chapter 4

THE VOICES THAT SHAPE YOU

Sieving Who and What You Hear

Chapter 5

THE DESTINYQUEEN OR THE DESTINY QUITTER

Owning and Wearing Your Crown for Destiny

Chapter 6

THE DESTINY PRESERVER OR DESTINY DESTROYER

Relocating and Realigning Yourself For Destiny

Dedication

I dedicate this book to every woman who is a Late Destiny Bloomer, a Destiny Dreamer and Chaser, a Destiny Spectator, a Destiny Gypsy, a Destiny Defector because ultimately each one of you has what it takes to become a Destiny Die-Hard.

Acknowledgement

First and foremost, I would like to thank God for enabling me to write and finish this Book Series. I pray these books will impact and bless many Women who are determined to fulfil their Destiny.

I would like to thank my **Husband Ngari** who really "gets me" and who I refer to as my "Destiny Spouse" because indeed he is a true gift from God and he has been supportive beyond measure during the course of my writing, these Books, in more ways than I can count.

My **sons Eric and Chris**, who are truly sons of my strength, and who have also supported and encouraged me in my "Destiny endeavours" no matter how radically insane I sounded at times.

My late **Dad, Chris Kahara** who constantly affirmed me and instilled the confidence I needed to embark on many "Destiny journeys" leading to where and who I am today.

Rev Teresa Wairimu, my "Destiny Midwife" who has spoken into my life for the past two decades and who has been diligent in nurturing, moulding and shaping me, to birth out the gifts within me (even during the times when my own foolishness and short-sightedness, coupled with a zeal that was often devoid of knowledge threatened to abort my Purpose and Calling.)

H.E. Madam Rachel Ruto who is equally passionate about the empowerment of women and who I admire and respect tremendously for her continuous and tireless commitment to better the lives of women in our society and Nation.

My Aunt Rev Judy Mbugua for believing in me and for being a pillar of strength to me for over the years as a Mother figure, for teaching me that my roles as a wife and mother are not an excuse for, but rather an incentive to fulfil my Purpose and Destiny.

My friend and Mentor Dr. Herta Von Stigel who came into my life, at just the right time and helped me to understand that I needed to conquer the Mountain within me before I could conquer the Mountains around me, and whose invaluable friendship and mentorship is a great source of encouragement for me.

My diligent research Assistants and Typists **Victor M. Mwangi**, **Frida Wanjira** and **Tecla Karimi** who all worked tirelessly in making these books happen.

My Publisher & Cover Designer Shadrack Radido of House Of Wealth Publishers who allowed me the freedom I needed in this Series of Books even when I stubbornly chose to deviate from the traditional Book writing ethics and who has been a solid sounding board on the many technical issues regarding this Series.

My Editor Dr. Mark Stibbe for his excellent editing and no-nonsense professional approach, truly a gift in the literary world.

My die-hard Spice Girls and faithful Women from my Seasoned Woman Vision who cheer me on and whose undeterred insistent claims that there is still more in me for them than I let out, warms my heart and provokes me to keep doing that which I was created for.

Everyone else who contributed in one way or another to the conception and birthing of this Series of Books.

Foreword

I have known Sally for over two decades now from the time she joined and begun to serve me in Ministry. Sally is a very zealous and passionate Woman in whatever she believes in.

Beyond her professional career as a Lawyer, Sally has demonstrated strong gifts of speaking, teaching, mentoring and writing and over the years I have often encouraged her to unleash these gifts. I am extremely proud to see that she has finally done so in these Books **"SEASONED FOR DESTINY"** and I am confident that she will go on to author many more for the benefit of this generation and the generations to come.

Sally has a distinct Call to the Women in the Marketplace for whom has an undeniable burden, and her ability to reach out and offer herself to those women who suffer in silence, totally closed up, yet they really need someone they can trust and open up to.

Sally has addressed every type of Woman in these Books and the topics and subjects she has chosen to address are of great interest so she will reach and impact a very wide margin of Women, across the divide, locally and globally.

In other words, Sally has covered literally every subject that every Woman needs, to become well equipped and empowered for fulfilling Purpose and Destiny. More importantly she has done it in a manner that every Woman will identify with, because she has delved into the core basics of every issue without sugar coating the seriousness that one will require to commit to this journey to Destiny. Yet at the same time she has strongly encouraged every Woman by laying out the road map and by affirming and assuring her again and again, that she already has what it takes to master this journey and fulfil her Destiny.

Women from every sphere and sector will be awakened to the significance of their Callings and Destiny, giving them the incentive and motivation, they needed to forge on without giving up.

I have been in Christian ministry for over 45 years now and I have been humbled and privileged to minister to thousands of people Worldwide and to lead an organization with over 10, 000 partners locally and globally. The messages in these Books are central to the gospel that I myself preach because Destiny is God ordained.

I have no doubt that everyone who will read these Books will be greatly impacted and transformed, empowered and equipped to arise and lay hold of and fulfil that Destiny that each was born for.

Rev. Teresia Wairimu Kinyanjui.

Director& Founder,

Faith Evangelistic Ministry (FEM).

Endorsement

Destiny is one of the most misunderstood concepts today. Needless to say, the very mention of this word elicits feelings of inadequacy and anxiety among many. This has mainly been because of the complexity and mystery that seems to surround the understanding of what destiny is or is not.

In the 'Seasoned for Destiny' series, Sally wholeheartedly deliberates on the tenets that are to bring flavor and color to one's life. Reading through the pages it is clear that she empties her heart seeking to touch a heart at a time. This series specifically address the internal struggles that become stumbling blocks in the way of success for many and in particular women.

In today's world where everything is fast-paced and we all are confronted with many options; it is prudent that one finds their space and balance in life. Reading this book will motivate you to take a personal stock of where you are in the journey to destiny while recognizing and fixing the hindrances on the way.

To live a life of meaning and significance understanding Destiny is not an option but an expectation. As one who is passionate about women empowerment, I concur that clarity of purpose and calling, the fortitude to make available connections and the resilience to maintain success on the path of destiny can be overwhelming. This series is therefore an essential tool for one to make this valuable journey.

Her Excellency,
Rachel Ruto.
Spouse of the Deputy President,
Republic of Kenya.

Endorsement

I have known Sally from when she was about 5 years old and our relationship is firstly that of a mother and daughter. Beyond our family ties and now that Sally has grown to be a wife and mother with her own home, we have become very close friends and prayer partners and we are a great support and strength to one another in this journey to Destiny.

From an early age, Sally has demonstrated such a strong gift of expression and articulation. Sally is undeniably a gifted and anointed Servant of God who ministers the gospel passionately. She is also an inspirational coach and mentor to many women and girls from every walk of life. Her marketplace ministry has impacted many far and wide.

When Sally birthed her Seasoned Woman Forum about 7 years ago and as I witnessed her teachings, mentorship and coaching programs, I knew it would just be a matter of time before she consolidated those valuable teachings into books to reach a wider audience and sphere.

I think that every woman reading this book who will be transformed radically and propelled to fulfilling her Purpose and Destiny.

I am very passionate for Families and Nations, and a firm believer that strong healthy families are the foundation of strong healthy Nations. So, as I read these Books, I was deeply affected and encouraged by the manner in which Sally has tied up the value of the woman, not only as a leader, wealth creator, professional, career woman, but also as a family-oriented woman.

Any woman serious about fulfilling her Purpose and Destiny must be able to align her role as a family woman with her Purpose and Destiny and she must be cognizant of the fact that she cannot effectively impact Nations without first impacting families.

This series of books addresses every woman of every race, creed and color, and from any society and Nation, who desires to be and do all that she was born and created for.

Sally has adequately highlighted literally every dilemma and problem that a woman will encounter in the course of fulfilling her Purpose and Destiny, irrespective of her social status and standing in life, and she has given very practical solutions to these dilemmas and problems.

I would therefore urge every woman to read this Series of Books not only for her own equipping and empowerment but also for the equipping and empowerment of other women who she will share the contents of these book with.

Rev. Dr. Judy Mbugua.

The Founder of the Homecare Spiritual Fellowship.

Endorsement

Sally Mahihu's book series *"Seasoned for Destiny"* is a clarion call for every woman, regardless of age, race or tribe, to discover her true identity, live out her deeper purpose and leave a legacy that younger generations are proud to remember. This book series is for such as time as this!"

Dr. Herta von Stiegel,

Author of *"The Mountain Within – Leadership Lessons and Inspiration for your Climb to the Top."*

Endorsement

I am glad that Sally has followed through in writing this series of books titled **"Seasoned for Destiny"**. A couple of years ago, I gave her a word which I had received from the lord, that she would write some very significant books on issues pertaining to women in the marketplace.

These books will encourage and guide women greatly in understanding certain fundamentals that are related to their destiny such as business, career, leadership, relationships etc. Sally has captured literally every aspect of a modern woman's life, and she has taken time to address and analyze these issues in a way that every woman can identify with.

Sally has left no stone unturned in candidly addressing the subtle and not so subtle issues that often derail and delay many women from unleashing their full potential, to enable them to bring out their best selves.

I am persuaded that these books will change the lives of many women and will equip a new generation to become powerful agents of transformation in their spheres of influence.

Rev. Steve Pailthorpe

President of Crown Global, CEO of Iconic Digital & Senior Pastor of Crown Family Church

Introduction

I am fully persuaded that once a Woman understands who she was born to be and embraces the reason she was created (the Purpose for her being), then she will begin to live purposefully and intentionally towards it, and attain true fulfilment. And in so doing she will not only lay hold of her own Destiny, but she will also impact and propel many people, societies and Nations to their Purpose and Destiny as well.

This Series known as *"Seasoned For Destiny"* consists of 5 Books namely Book 1 Your Naming And Defining, Book 2 Your Calling And Positioning, Book 3 Your Relationships And Networks, Book 4 Your Making And Shaping and Book 5 Your Harvests And Legacy.

BOOK 1 titled **"YOUR NAMING AND DEFINING"** deals with a Woman's identity, understanding **"the who"** she was born to be, it addresses her ability to embrace her true and authentic self. The chapters in this Book expound the various fundamentals regarding Identity and the power of Naming; The

Passwords to your true identity (understanding what should and what should not define you). The Triggers to an Identity Crisis, The Diary of a Destiny Diva, The Voices that shape and define you, The Destiny Queen or the Destiny Quitter, The Destiny Preserver or the Destiny Destroyer, The Destiny Clinger or the Destiny Kisser, The Destiny Connector or the Destiny Blocker, The Global Destiny Carrier or the Local Destiny Carrier, The Destiny Respecter or the Destiny Despiser, The Eagle Destiny or the Chicken Destiny, The Diary of a Destiny Diva and The Daily Confessions of a Destiny Chaser (on how to reinforce and affirm your identity daily with positive decrees and declarations).

BOOK 2 titled **"YOUR CALLING AND POSITIONING"** deals with a Woman's Calling and Purpose namely how to discover **"the what"** she was created to do, how to birth it and safeguard it, having a deep insight of what her purpose and calling entails, understanding how to access what she needs to fulfil it. This Book also it looks at the Woman's Positioning and Alignment on how to locate **"the where"** (in terms of sector or sphere) she is ordained to impact, how to navigate in that specific area and how to establish herself there. The chapters in this particular Book address the pertinent factors about Calling and Positioning namely; The Cues and Clues to her Calling, The Realities About her Calling, The Tools of a true Visionary, The steps to Birthing her Visions to Destiny, The Steps after Birthing her Visions to Destiny, The Pebble Stones in your High Heels to Destiny, The Arrows to her Place and sphere, The Snags and Snares in her Place and sphere, Establishing herself in the Place of Assignment and The Key Roles Of A Destiny Woman.

BOOK 3 titled "**YOUR RELATIONSHIPS AND NETWORKS**" deals with a Woman's relationships (networks and associations) namely "**the whom**" she should connect to, or disconnect from, for the sake of her Destiny. The chapters in this Book address; The Paradoxes In A Destiny Woman, Your Destiny Helpers, Your Destiny Killers, Your Sibling Rivals, Mastering The Art of Negotiation, The Spice Girls and Your Suspect Suitors.

BOOK 4 titled "**YOUR MAKING AND SHAPING**" deals with a Woman's moulding and sculpturing for Destiny namely "**the How**" of her preparation and equipping, and the various tests and trials she needs to undergo in order to fulfil her Purpose and Call as well as the principles, values and habits that inform her choices and decisions and refine her for Destiny. The chapters in this Book address and include; The Storms of a Destiny Survivor, The Scars of a Sculptured Woman, The Pain Patterns of a Destiny Champion, The Shape of a Destiny Diamond, The Trademarks of a Destiny Vessel, The Habits of a Destiny Addict, The Elegance of an Eagle Woman and The Pit-stops of a Destiny Racer.

BOOK 5 titled "**YOUR HARVESTS AND LEGACY**" deals with a Woman's legacy and the footprints she leaves behind for her generation and future generations. The chapters in this Book include; The Seasons Of a Destiny Sower, Your Harvest In 7 Areas, Facts About Your Harvest, Hindrances To Your Harvest, Threats To Your Harvest, How To Respond To Your Harvest, Reasons Why You Get The Harvest, The Purpose Of Your Harvest, The Marks Of A Destiny Legend and A Woman's Defining Decades.

One of the main reasons for writing this Book was to consolidate the Principles that I have been teaching, coaching and mentoring on over the years with regard to Purpose and Destiny.

Perhaps another compelling reason for writing this Series of Books is that every issue addressed here resonates within me personally, because these are issues I or people very close to me, continue to grapple with, and my sharing them here is for purposes of identifying my own personal struggles with those of the women I am addressing.

It is my sincere desire and hope that those who read this Series of Books will use the teachings to propel themselves to Destiny and to pass them on to other women, including those they are training, mentoring and coaching.

These Books will also form very valuable material for discussion groups whether as Book clubs, diverse groups within churches, corporate organizations and in all the various sectors and spheres of influence and hence the reason I have inserted "Destiny questions to ponder on" at the end of each chapter so that the interactive discussions can have a real impact on each reader and hopefully provoke them to apply the guidelines offered here in fulfilling their Purpose and Calling.

My sincere hope and expectation is that these Books are going to equip and empower every Woman desirous of fulfilling Purpose and to edify and assure her that no matter how hard the journey has been and no matter how much she has wanted to give up, she indeed has what it takes to finish this journey because she was designed for Destiny and she is already seasoned for it.

Although the target audience of this Series is primarily Women, it is now clear to me that even the men who come across them it will be equally impacted and equipped by the universal principles and the various topics addressed.

It is also my intention to target the young woman (older teens and young adults) because most of these principles and issues will greatly help these young women to avoid the mistakes that many of us older women made in our early years, and it will hopefully help the young woman to also avoid unnecessary delays in her journey to Destiny. It is therefore my sincere hope and prayer that every woman, young and old will read this Series of Books and be propelled to her Destiny.

The most fundamental aspect when embarking on your journey to Destiny is knowing **"the who you were born to be"** and coming to a place where you embrace your true and authentic self and walk securely in it because everything else thereafter regarding your Destiny hinges on this first revelation about your true self-identity.

These Books address, every Woman at whatever place she may be in her quest for Purpose and Destiny, the late Destiny bloomer, the Destiny dreamer and Destiny chaser, the Destiny wagon, the Destiny spectator, the Destiny backslider.

These Women are all desirous of living purposefully but they each struggle with different aspects about Destiny, whereby some may struggle with knowing and discovering 'the who' and 'the what' they were created to be (their self-identity and Calling), they go round in circles seeking 'the where' they were assigned to influence (their place and sphere of assignment) and 'the whom' they were designed to relate and connect with (the relationships), many of them get blindsided by the how they get made and formed (tests, trials and tribulations), while others navigate life steering dangerously without a road map seeking '**the which**' (values and principles) they need to get there, while others become lethargic and burnout because they lack a sufficient conviction that the journey is worth the high price and sacrifice, they seem to be paying.

Every Woman's future after reading this Series of Books will be brightened by her assurance and confidence that she can now become the who she was born to be, do the what she was created to do, locate and position herself where she was sent to be an influence, relate and connect with the people that were assigned for her, surrender and embrace the process that will mould and make her into a vessel fit for Destiny, walk and align with the principles and values that she was intended to use to usher her to Destiny, lay hold of and effectively manage the successes, rewards and harvests that come with her faithfulness and diligence and leave footprints that will be a positive legacy for her generation and future generations.

What Is to be Seasoned For Destiny ?

For Purposes of this series of Books being "**Seasoned**" does not mean you have accomplished and "**arrived**" rather it means that you are passionate enough to lay hold of your Destiny, that you are ready to step forth by faith and embark on this epic journey just as you are; with the assurance that as you do so, the equipping and empowering you seek or need will be part and parcel of the journey.

... "**Being Seasoned for Destiny**" means that even though you occasionally struggle with who you are in the midst of a tumultuous dispensation that often seeks to swallow and drown you... **YET** you tenaciously fight to keep your head up, knowing that there is only one of you, and the only one you need to be, the one you were born to be.

... **"Being Seasoned for Destiny"** means that even though there are many raw and rough edges in your Character, that are still undergoing moulding and shaping... **YET** you continue to submit yourself to the skilful hands of the Master Potter, knowing that a **"Choice Vessel"** like you, will take longer to be formed because of the great impact and influence you will have on Nations and Generations.

... **"Being Seasoned for Destiny"** means that even though you have not quite mastered the Storms of life like failed relationships, chronic failures, loneliness, self-doubt and rejection, just to mention a few... **YET** you continue to brace yourself against those storms, choosing to dance in the rain; knowing that as you continue to set your sail in the wind of hope then ultimately, those storms will in fact become the very forces that will strengthen and propel you and bring you to that higher place of being alone, but not lonely, a place of self-knowledge, self-acceptance and self-assurance.

.... **"Being Seasoned for Destiny"** means that even though the seed of your womb has not germinated into the **"Daughters of Substance"** and **"Sons of Strength"** you had hoped for... **YET** you remain expectant that irrespective of any shortcomings in your parenting skills, or any unjust twist of fate, your resilience as a praying mother is never in vain and in due season, your Sons and Daughters will manifest into a Seasoned Generation, that will shake cities and impact Nations.

... **"Being seasoned for Destiny"** means that even though you may constantly be in a financial mess and distress, until you feel so desperate and drained... **YET** you refuse to despair knowing that your hands are anointed to create wealth and as you continue to trust, embrace and practice sound godly wealth creating habits and principles, then surely the floodgates of heaven will fling open and usher you into unprecedented financial freedom.

... **"Being Seasoned for Destiny** "means that even though the dire consequences of your **poor choices**, have come to haunt you and you are paying the painful price of your past folly under a heavy cloak of remorse... **YET** you keep your head lifted up high knowing that as you appreciate the lessons learned from your past folly, then this too will pass; because your harsh and ugly Winter must ultimately surrender to your soft and beautiful Spring that will come with forbearance and Second Chances.

... **"Being Seasoned for Destiny"** means that perhaps your inner joy is being dampened by the anguish and agony of a sick body.... **YET** you forge on, smiling through your pain knowing that as long as you have a Purpose and Assignment, that you are committed to fulfil and a Destiny to lay hold of, then your Creator will preserve you and keep you, until you are done.

...**"Being Seasoned for Destiny"** means that even though your walk with God is like a seesaw, characterised by some seasons of intense (almost fanatical) passion and commitment and a radical faith, but also with other seasons of panic, doubt, or even silent indignation when things do not go the way you thought... **YET** you pick yourself up every time and dust off the doubt and purge your panic, and with hot blinding tears, you make a decision to hope and trust anyway, knowing that He who began a good work in you is able to complete it.

...**"Being Seasoned For Destiny"** means that even though you have encountered Chronic failures and disappointment... **YET** it is about finding the grace to deal with the many disappointments of life and finding the resolve to regain missed seasons and lost opportunities, it is about finding the strength to reposition yourself for a new beginning, because a Seasoned Woman knows, that while there is life, there is hope and while there is hope, there is always another chance to rise again and forge on to fulfil her Destiny.

… **"Being Seasoned for Destiny"** means that even though you come to the end of yourself **YET** your find a song in your heart that keeps you going when the journey gets tough and this is the song that will keep her going even when the storms rage and the fiery furnace flares.

The Seasoned Woman knows…

Who she really is…

The Purpose for which she was created…

She is uniquely gifted…

She does not allow her failures…

And successes to define her…

She confidently says…

When I grow up, I want to be Me!

The Seasoned Woman knows…

She is fearfully and wonderfully made…

With a true beauty inside her…

Reflected in her whole life lived…

The Seasoned Woman clothes herself…

In dignity, honesty, integrity, patience, kindness, mercy and love…

The Seasoned Woman has learnt…

To embrace the seasons of her life…

Allow them to mould and sculpt her…

Into a vessel of strength, honour and dignity…

She is a Woman of all Seasons…

A vessel of strength, honour and dignity…

She has learnt to weather and survive the storms of her daily life…

Having the grace to dance in the rain…

To smile through her pain…

She has risen to define life…

The strength to rise like a phoenix from the ashes…

The Seasoned Woman has passion for her Nation…

She has solutions for her Generation…

And she has the welfare of her people at heart…

She is a voice to the voiceless…

So, as you reflect and take stock of all the myriad of Seasons you may have encountered so far in your journey to Destiny, remember that you are **"So Totally Seasoned"** for your Destiny and that nothing shall by any means prevent you, from finishing your Race and not only finishing it, but finishing strong… so soldier on **Woman of Destiny**, until you reach the finish line.

Chapter One

IDENTIFIED FOR DESTINY

Understanding "The Who" You Were Born To Be and Embracing Your True Identity

Chapter Preview

A) Understanding Your Identity

1. *The Woman who does not know "the who" she was born to be.*

2. *The Woman who rejects "the who" she was born to be.*

3. *The Woman who is "the who" that others want her to be.*

4. *The Woman who allows circumstances, adversity and her past to dictate "the who" she is.*

5. *The Woman who misrepresents "the who" she should be to get ahead.*

6. *The Woman who allows transient things to determine "the who" she is.*

7. *The Woman who allows her ego to define "the who" she is.*

B) Aligning Your True Identity with Your Name

1. *Your name is what you answer to.*

2. *Your name comes loaded with baggage whether good or bad.*

3. *The power in your name propels and directs you.*

4. *You can make your name submit to your true identity.*

5. *Namelessness can arise from several scenarios.*

6. *Your name can be changed to align with who you really are and where you want to go.*

7. *Your true name should be the one God calls you by.*

UNDERSTANDING YOUR IDENTITY

Your identity is foundational to your destiny. Knowing your identity determines your destiny because once you realize who you were born to be, this gives you a whole new perspective and guides your direction towards what you were born to do. Identity is therefore not just who you are currently but who you are called to become.

It is significant to note that many heroes, once they came to a revelation of *the who* they were born to be, experienced a paradigm shift and set off in the right direction towards their destiny. As someone once wrote, "Life isn't about discovering yourself; it's about finding out who God created you to be."

"Are you *the who* you were born to be?" This question presupposes or suggests that it is possible to discover that you are not *the who* you were born to be. Perhaps your current self is a pale shadow or a total distortion, or even a tragic misrepresentation of *the who* you are supposed to be. Knowing our real identity gives us security, strengthens our character, gives us self-esteem, reveals our uniqueness, individuality, distinctiveness and leads to a healthy self-awareness, which leads to self-love and self-acceptance.

The phrase, *the who you were born to be* could imply that you may be living either as *the who* you think you were born to be, living as *the who* you want to be, or living as *the who* that people say you should be. Who are you when you are not so busy being who other people want you to be? Are you perhaps making misguided attempts to be everyone instead of the one woman you were born to be? These are some of the questions Bishop T. D. Jakes poses in his book *The Leading Woman*. This process of discovery is vital because, as Vironika Tugaleva writes, *"You will never know who you are unless you shed who you pretend to be."*

If you are to reach your destiny, one of the most fundamental assignments you will have to undertake is to define who you are and who you were born to be. You must sacrifice *the who* you would like to be if you are to be *the who* you were born to be.

Very often we seek to be who we are not because it is more exciting and more comfortable, involving fewer responsibilities and less challenges. However, you can never fulfil your destiny unless you embrace *the who* you were born to be. Richard Grant says, **"The value of identity of course is that so often with it comes purpose."** When your true identity is locked within you, muzzled and suffocated, you will constantly suffer from an intense inner wrestling and a small nagging voice, questioning your identity. This struggle will intensify until you release yourself into your true identity and become secure in who you really are. Once you agree to let go of all false identities and wrong labels, then you are on your way to finding and acquiring your true identity. In the meantime, you may experience inner turmoil. As Bryant McGill says, **"All discomfort comes from suppressing your true identity."**

Your true identity is an inner reality and can be defined as "the best version of yourself." It is your authentic self – the self where your words and actions are consistent and aligned. Authenticity denotes integrity, honesty, transparency, and openness. Authenticity is the daily practice of letting go of who you think you are supposed to be and embracing who you really are. Let go of who you think you need to be and embrace who you were born to be.

Many are fearful of being authentic because authenticity makes you vulnerable. Authenticity requires exposing your imperfect dysfunctional self to others, risking unkind feedback. Suffice it to say that people's opinions should not hinder you from embracing your authentic self, no matter how exposed it will make you feel. Your incentive should be the fact that authenticity promotes a healthy relationship with yourself, which then determines the health of all your other relationships. This is a prize worth seeking!

Knowing and defining *the who* you were born to be is a prerequisite to discovering, embracing, and fulfilling *the why* you were created (your life purpose). Your identity, your *being*, must come before your purpose or *doing* because your true identity or *being* is what unlocks your abilities and the potential to fulfil your purpose.

Your successes or failures, wealth or poverty, beauty or fame may help to shape your destiny, but they do not define your identity. You must understand that though these may express your identity, they do not form it. Never suffocate your extraordinary self and your unique identity by restricting them to transient things. One woman gave the following "emotional nutrition" to her daughter:

"I will tell you, daughter of mine, every day of your worth and not of your beauty, because your beauty is given, and every being is born beautiful, but knowing your worth can save your life. Raising you on beauty alone, you will be starved, you will be raw, you will be weak, an easy stomach always in need of someone to tell you how beautiful you are. So, let your worth, not your beauty, define you."

You are also not defined by your pain or mistakes. Your mistakes are not final, so don't let them hold you hostage. Beware of creating negative narratives about yourself by allowing wrong things to define you.

When it comes to the struggles with identity, many women fall into at least one of seven categories:

1. The woman who does not know *"the who"* she was born to be.

She is the one who has no knowledge whatsoever of her true identity because she has no revelation and knowledge of the Maker who holds the "creation certificate" and "identity card" that disclose who she was born to be. Sadly, she does not even realize that she is without a real identity, so she carries on with her life adopting any identity imposed upon her by those around her or by society generally, even though their defining of her does not bear witness deep within to who she is meant to be. Consequently, she will be restless and unfulfilled no matter how seemingly successful she may look on the outside because deep inside is a hollow emptiness, one she cannot explain. She hears about destiny and even desires it but is unable to embark on it because her lack of authentic identity keeps holding her back. She needs to learn what Aristotle discovered, that *"knowing yourself is the beginning of all wisdom."*

This woman's captivity will be broken on the day her restlessness and anguish become unbearable and she decides to embark on a quest for self-discovery. When she comes to the knowledge of her Creator, in whom her identity is rooted, He discloses to her the passwords to unlock her true identity. This sets her on her journey to destiny.

2. The woman who rejects *"the who"* she was born to be

This is the woman who has sufficient knowledge of her Creator and even knows the identity given her. However, whether consciously or subconsciously, she rejects this identity, possibly because of the responsibility that comes with it, one she is not ready to embrace, or because that identity does not reflect how she sees herself or how she lives her life. In other words, there is a disconnect between *the who* she was born to be and *the who* she currently is. As a result, she has forgotten the uniqueness of her identity – that she is an original, one of a kind, and not a copy – and instead she chooses to imitate others whom she admires, or who she considers better than herself – hence her insecurity in her own identity. She wants to be every other woman but herself.

She needs to stop using someone else's identity card and must own and embrace her own uniqueness and her own true identity.

3. **The woman who is** *"the who"* **that others want her to be**.

This is the woman who starts off with a very clear knowledge and revelation of her identity, and the One in whom it is rooted, but over time several factors gang up against her, suffocating her true identity, until she subconsciously gives in and becomes who others want her to be in order to serve their agenda. These others may not even do this with any ill intent, because most of them may be her loved ones – her spouse, children, parents, friends, associates, employers, superiors – whose expectations and demands of her become overwhelming. The stress and strains that comes with the many roles this woman plays, along with her responsibilities, can and often do cloud over her true identity and these roles begin to define her even though they should not. This woman must shed and cast off every wrong label imposed on her if she is to become *the who* she was born to be.

4. The woman who allows circumstances, adversity, and her past to dictate *"the who"* she is.

This is the woman who has been battered by the storms of life and suffers from past pains and failures. She struggles with her many roles and responsibilities which, in turn, have formed her into *the who* she has become. She may also have suffered, or continues to suffer, from various types of abuse - physical, emotional, social, financial - which viciously eat at her self-esteem and completely erode any true sense of self. This woman must address and confront everything that suffocates and distorts her true identity if she has any hope of fulfilling her destiny. She must do this by letting go of all bitterness, anger, doubt, disbelief, disappointments, pain, and woundedness. She must learn to master her storms and manage her different roles so that they do not define her.

5. The woman who misrepresents *"the who"* she is to get ahead.

This is the woman who adopts a fake identity because she believes it will get her ahead in life. She is motivated by greed and self-serving agendas and feels the need to be popular and accepted. So, driven by this approval addiction, she poses with beliefs, values, and views that she knows will give her the right image to get what she wants. However, her pretence and hypocrisy become her biggest limitations because you can never be effective without being authentic. This adopting of false identities is very common in the marketplace, and more so in the corporate sector, although it is usually clothed and camouflaged with words and phrases such as *emotional intelligence, leverage, mapping, posturing* or *strategizing*, which sugar coats what you know is wrong and deceptive. And deception is the goal here. The objective of adopting a false identity is always to deceive other people into thinking you are who you are not. This woman is like a teenage girl using a fake ID to get into a club for over 21-year-olds. The ID is a deception. Your true identity is the only identity that empowers you to fulfil your destiny. You must be secure in your true identity. If there are elements that defile your identity so that you become ashamed of it and therefore seek a fake identity then it is your duty to reject and resist these defilements and keep your identity pure and true. As someone has said, *"Be careful who you pretend to be; you might forget who you are."*

6. The woman who allows transient things to determine *"the who"* she is.

This is the woman who sincerely but erroneously believes that her identity is derived from things such as her success and accomplishments, her career, roles, positions and powers, her wealth and material substance, her social status or physical appearances, fashion sense and beauty. The problem is these things are transient and as soon as they shift, which they must over time, then her identity is totally shaken, and she ends up in an identity crisis. This leads to her compounding her misconception by beginning to define herself by her failures and flaws, lack, rejection. This woman must seek to understand the criteria that should define her and the things that should not.

7. The woman who allows her ego to define "the who" she is.

This is the woman who either has an inflated sense of self, an exaggerated sense of self-importance, worth, value, and grandiosity – or the woman who has such a low sense of self-value and esteem that she undermines and belittles herself. The woman with too big an ego possesses a distorted identity which makes her prideful and unteachable. She denies that her identity is rooted in God and instead she roots her identity in self. Conversely, the woman with too low an ego also possesses a distorted identity which makes her timid, lacking in confidence, and prone to a victim syndrome. The chances are that both these women - the one bloated by her self-acclaimed perfection, accomplishments, success, titles, and positions, and the one suffocated by her own flaws and imperfections, failures, and dysfunctions - are both covering up deep-seated issues and insecurities, or they are adopting a defence mechanism against rejection, fear of failure, criticism, and condemnation. This woman must shed her false mind-set if she is to discover her true identity.

As Frederick Lenz said, **"The ego is a false perception of self. It is an idea, a transitory identity that we have picked up."**

ALIGNING YOUR TRUE IDENTITY TO YOUR NAME

There are seven important things to consider about the connection between your name and your identity because often the two are regarded as synonymous. In what follows, we will look at seven important things you need to understand about your name and your identity:

- You need to understand what name you answer to
- You need to understand what baggage - whether good or bad - your name comes with
- You need to understand that the power in your name propels and directs you towards, or away from, your purpose, calling, and destiny
- You need to understand that you can change your name to align with what you want to be and where you want to go

- You need to understand that the lack of a name often leads to a lack of identity
- You need to understand that you can decide whether your name should define you or not
- You need to understand that your true name should be the one which God calls you. If you sincerely believe that He is your Creator, then He is the one with the mandate to define and name you.

1) Your Name Is What You Answer To

W. C. Fields said, *"It isn't what they call you; it's what you answer to."*

It is possible to discover your identity through your name because when you were a child, or later in life, a sense of identity may have been conveyed in and through your name. As a parent, you should want your child to carry a name of significance that embodies a destiny and a legacy. You must be intentional and deliberate when naming your child, or when naming yourself, should you have an opportunity to do so. When you were born, you may have been given and ascribed an identity through your name, one about which you had no say. You answer to your name, confirming that you are who and what your name means. Your name identifies and defines you by setting you apart and distinguishing you from others. A name can often be symbolic, pointing to some virtue or quality. Think of names like Faith, Grace, Hope, Victor, Patience; these carry great significance for determining who you are and what you are called to embody.

It is believed that a name can shape a person's character, mould their social identity, and even influence their destiny. The meaning attached to a name will determine much about the present and the future of a child.

One can also often infer someone's socio-cultural background from their name, including their ethnicity, gender, day or date of birth, family's occupation, social and political class, the religion and deities they follow, and the hopes and dreams of their parents.

A name can also express the values, ethics, and beliefs of the culture into which the child has been born.

The name of a child can also signify other things: the unique circumstances in which the child was born; the day they were born; the important natural, social, or historical events that were happening at the time of their birth; how many siblings were born before them; the primary occupation or social class of the family. These factors all naturally give rise to descriptive names. So, for example, children may be named according to the day of the week, the time of the day or the season when they were born. They may be named following the order in which they were born in the particular family, the circumstances of the birth of the child, whether it was a premature birth or a normal one, the circumstances of the family and the community, and important events. The material wealth of the family may be reflected in the names selected by the parents for their children.

A name also reflects an entire society's ethical framework, reinforcing the values that it holds, placing on its members the responsibility to live up to the value denoted by their name. For example, in some communities, names are used as a way of informing one's enemies that a person is aware of some evil scheme that is used against him, such as sorcery.

Some names come with titles or positions so as you answer to that name you are in essence accepting and embracing the meaning and functions of that title - for example, Pastor, Bishop, Doctor, Mrs., Miss, Mother of, Daughter of, Teacher,

Chief, Your Excellency, Honourable, Professor, to name just a few.

Many names reflect the attributes of God; they express praise or thanksgiving to God. Many children are named after the deceased members of the family.

Some names refer to the state of health of the new-born baby and their physical features. Some children may be given several names, depending upon the custom of the community. Other names by which one is known may be added at a later stage, particularly as the result of going through rituals of initiation.

Names usually have a meaning. In them you can see a connection with the past. You can be named after ancestors and given names that point to the future. Names can serve as a kind of manifesto for what you are supposed to implement in your life at a later stage.

In addition to all of this, the naming process has traditionally played a vital role in the life of the community. Various members were involved in this at various stages - parents, family, elders, friends.

In short, when you answer to your name, you are answering to what that name means, symbolizes, or represents. You must come to understand this. Then you can either choose to change your name to a more amenable one, or, by embracing salvation in Christ and have any negative connotations in your name cleansed by the blood of Jesus.

2) Your Name Comes Loaded With Baggage Whether Good Or Bad

Uri Simonsohn said, *"Names tell us a lot about who you are."*

Your name links you to characteristics, qualities and personality traits that distinguish you from others. These names can affect your self-esteem, self-confidence, self-awareness, habits, behaviour, and reputation, giving you a label, whether good or bad. They can also produce stigmas, depending on what associations they have. For example, it is virtually impossible to call a boy "Adolf" now without it being associated with Hitler. If you come to be given that name, it will be hard for others not to attach negative ideas to your identity. Where the name you are given at birth, or the name you may give yourself knowingly as an adult, points to certain negative characteristics and traits, this has usually happened because.

That name is associated with a famous historical figure who bore it, or still bears it if they are still alive - someone who demonstrated those characteristics and traits, say a robber, a murderer, a child molester, a dictator, a cult leader etc.

It could be the name of a relative, whether deceased or still alive, who is associated with certain bad characteristics.

It could be a Biblical name also associated with certain characteristics like Judas Iscariot, Mary Magdalene, Jezebel etc.

It is difficult for you to become disassociated from the characteristics implied by such names unless you demonstrate such radical, opposite traits that this completely counters and nullifies the negative connotations of your name.

Likewise, your name may come loaded with positivity. You may be named after an historical figure, family member or biblical character that symbolizes noble characteristics with which you are then associated, unless, that is, you somehow demonstrate the opposite so radically that the virtues implied by that name are completely forgotten.

The negative implications that come with a name not only include labels, stigmas, character flaws, but in some cultures, names can be linked with a particular animal and its behaviours, which may lead us to live out those traits, either knowingly or unknowingly. Some people are named after places that have a negative reputation, and the people so named may embody its traits either knowingly or unknowingly. If you're named "**Vegas**", don't be surprised if you start having a problem with gambling later on in your life. If you're called "**Oasis**", don't be surprised if people gather around you because you have a refreshing personality.

It is interesting to note how accurately the names of people in the Bible matched their personalities. Jacob means trickster. David means man after God's heart. This shows that you carry whatever your name denotes, unless or until you decide to change it.

A name is implicitly associated with certain characteristics and people use these associations however unknowingly to make judgements about the competence and suitability of its bearer. Maybe the better question is not what is in a name, but rather what signals does my name send and what does it imply?

A name allows people to make snap judgements and assumptions about us. While this can be harmful, names can also provide the fastest way to know about someone and their social context. This tells us how to interact with that person.

Your name, together with what it denotes, is the first impression people get about you. It is the first window they open onto your life, even before they begin to judge how you dress, how you wear your hair, how you behave and talk. Your name must therefore be something you take seriously. You must analyze it to ensure it does not carry any negative labels that may cause people to write you off even before they have met the real you.

A woman who is born out of two different cultures – say, for example, where one parent is white and from the West and the other is from Africa or Asia - may bear a name from one culture and another name from the other culture. She may be very selective which name she chooses to use in which context, depending on how she believes the people will perceive her. Whether your name indicates your culture, religion, or gender, it influences how you present yourself to the world and how you interact with the world.

Your naming at birth is therefore critical because the name you are given suggests what you will be associated with, whether a virtue, a place, or a person. From there, it is possible that we grow and develop in the spirit of our name.

As Kelley Armstrong says, *"A name is so important. A surname connects you to your past, to your family. Even a given name has meaning - why did your parents pick that particular one?"* Logan Pearsall Smith says, *"Our names are labels, plainly printed on the bottle, the essence of our past behaviour."*

3) The Power In Your Name Propels And Directs You *"Names Have Power,"* says Rick Riordan.

It goes without saying that there is power in a name. The name of a person can influence, direct, pull or propel them towards a certain way, towards certain choices and inclinations. We often hear how a name can have psychological effects. A woman's name can influence:

- *Her choice of career or profession, where she lives, her marriage preferences etc.*
- *Her academic achievements and performance in the workplace.*
- *How she will be treated by teachers and professors at school or by her superiors and peers in the workplace – treatment that may affect her life overall.*

Your name may impact and have power to direct the course of your life in terms of your choices, decisions, actions, and your traits. Thus, your name may have the power to direct you and shape you in a particular manner and path. Your name can either form and direct you towards or away from your destiny. To that extent it matters what you answer to and what identity you choose to embrace.

When your naming is well informed, your name and your identity should direct and usher you to your destiny. Where your naming is ill-informed and ill-intended, then this can derail you from your destiny unless you take necessary action to stop it from doing so. It is therefore easy to understand why names in the Bible often described the person's birth, characteristics, circumstances, and call. Moses's name means "drawn out of the water" or "deliverer." Peters means "Rock." Jacob means "trickster." Abraham means "Father of many nations." Your name and your identity, when they align, provide a fundamental key to your destiny because knowing who you are is related to knowing what purpose you have on this earth to fulfil. Being secure in this is one of the signs that you are seasoned for destiny.

4) You Can Make Your Name Submit To Your True Identity

If your name is deemed synonymous with your identity, if it carries certain traits worthy of association, and if your name has the power to direct and propel you in a certain direction - especially in line with your purpose, calling, and destiny - then it goes without saying that you must make a decision as to whether you want to allow your name (especially when it was given to you and you had no choice over it) to define you and affect you, or whether you want to take on your true identity and let your name submit to that identity.

Since our names and identities describe who we are and are a representation of how we perceive ourselves – and how others perceive us – then it is important to understand the link between your name and your identity and to what extent your name may be betraying your true identity. Every person's name holds some special meaning. For example, your naming may have been influenced by the following factors:

- You may have been named after a family member to show respect or honour to their memory, irrespective of the baggage that those family members may carry with them, good or bad.
- Your name may have been given in accordance with your culture, for example, in line with the tradition that a firstborn son is named after his father's father, and a firstborn daughter is named after her father's mother.
- You may have been named in a culture where names are given according to seasons, events, or the time of birth (night, day, rainy season, summer etc)
- You may have been named in a culture where naming evolves according to the age of the person, where some are named at childhood, others at adolescence and others at adulthood.
- You may have been named after a famous, gifted person like a scientist, a leader, a historian, a gifted musician, or artist.

Your name may well have been given by your parents, culture or society and it may therefore not be identity enhancing. Sometimes, the names others give to us can become unhelpful labels that point to unfair stereotypes, and this in turn can negatively impact our identity. When this happens, it is important to realize that your name is one of the critical factors in establishing not only your sense of identity but your awareness of destiny. You may need to consider choosing a name for yourself that is not based on your relationships and roles, nor on your work and status, nor on your religion and faith, but something deeper. Ignoring the power in your name to direct you in a certain direction may have some effect on your ability to fulfil your purpose, calling, and destiny. *"Names are powerful and so is destiny, but a person's will is more powerful than both put together"* **(Liesl Shurtliff).**

5) Namelessness Can Arise From Several Scenarios

Everybody has a name, whether it is perceived to be a good or a bad name, and that name comes with an identity. However, in some instances, such as when someone is incarcerated, their name is taken away and replaced with a number. In the process of stripping that person of their name, they are also deprived of the identity that comes with that name. Whether or not the reasoning behind this is justified, it can have some very adverse and long-lasting effects on a person because this process denudes them of dignity, individuality, and identity. A person in this scenario can become identity-less. Years later, they must begin a journey of self-discovery to remember who they were born to be and thereby lay hold of their true identity.

Here is another scenario. As a married woman, you may take on the name of your husband and, over time, if you are not careful, you may begin to lose your identity. A time may then come when you can only be defined as "the wife of so-and-so." Likewise, if you have children, you may be referred to as "the mother of so-and-so." Again, if you are not careful, a time may come when you are only defined by the relationships, roles, and responsibilities of your new life. In short, you must be careful that you do not allow your roles to be the ultimate and determining factor in establishing your true sense of identity.

This derives from something deeper than that.

6) Your Name Can Be Changed To Align With Who You Really Are And Where You Want To Go

William Shakespeare said, *"What's in a name? That which we call a rose, by any other name would smell as sweet."*

After marriage, a woman usually changes her last name to signify the beginning of the next chapter of her life and this gives her an identity which should be an addition to her existing identity. It should *not* be a replacement. However, a wife may over time lose her identity and be defined according to her role. This can lead to an identity crisis where she forgets who she was born to be and what she was created to do. This is even more so after a divorce where she must rediscover and redefine herself afresh.

In the Bible, we find many situations where God changes someone's given name. It is important to understand what would lead God to take such a drastic step. In each case, God wanted to instill a new vision for that person's life, a new role and purpose that He wanted them to fulfil. Here are some examples.

God changed Abram's name to Abraham to reflect the shift in Abraham's role from a father figure in a limited family context to a father figure to an entire nation. In **Genesis 17:4–6**, we read this:

"As for Me, behold, my covenant is with you, and you shall be a father of many nations. No longer shall your name be called Abram, but your name shall be Abraham; for I have made you a father of many nations. I will make you exceedingly fruitful; and I will make nations of you, and kings shall come from you."

God also changed Sarai's name to Sarah to reflect the fact that she grew into a woman who trusts God's promises and was no longer a woman scoffing at God's promises in disbelief. We read in **Genesis 17:15-16:**

"Then God said to Abraham, 'As for Sarai your wife, you shall not call her name Sarai, but Sarah *shall be* her name. And I will bless her and also give you a son by her; then I will bless her, and she shall be *a mother of* nations; kings of peoples shall be from her'."

God changed Peter's name from Shimon (Simon) meaning *"God has heard"* into Peter whose name meant *"a pillar of strength and a rock."* Eventually, Peter lived up to his name. As Jesus says in **Matthew 16:18-19:**

"And I also say to you that you are Peter, and on this rock, I will build My church, and the gates of Hades shall not prevail against it. And I will give you the keys of the kingdom of heaven, and whatever you bind on earth will be bound in heaven, and whatever you loose on earth will be loosed in heaven."

God changed Jacob's name which meant "deceiver," *"one who supplants another,"* to Israel *("one who wrestles/ triumphs with God")* and from then on, his life changed and the blessings that came with the name Israel rested upon him **(Genesis 32:22-28).**

God changed somebody's name in the Bible when He was about to give them a new assignment, or usher them into their real purpose and destiny. He did this by removing the connotations that their earlier name and identity conveyed (which were sometimes negative or diminishing), giving them a new name with a positive nuance.

As we grow from one age to another, our identity evolves and matures so the name and identity that you may have had at 15-years-old may be very different from the name and identity you will have at 25 or 50. As we grow, change, and have new experiences, what we called ourselves when we were younger may not be what we call ourselves now. You may have called yourself "Tabby" in kindergarten, but on transitioning to adulthood you may change your name to "Tabitha" to reflect your new sense of maturity and identity.

Depending on the situation, what we call ourselves may change as our sense of identity develops over time. What once resonated with us no longer chimes with our sense of identity, which has evolved as part of a complex process. Self-discovery is a progressive and continuous journey through various stages, steps, insights, "aha" moments, that add up to a broader and clearer picture of self. So, as you constantly evaluate your name and identity, you could ask yourself this question: is it different from what it was 15 years ago? Do you think that it will be different 15 years from now?

7) Your true name should be the one God calls you

David Jeremiah said, *"Names can be a doorway into knowing who a person is, and that is certainly true of God. A study of His names is a study of who He is and will be for you"*.

If you believe that you are God's creation and God's child, then you will also believe that He is the one that holds your true name and identity. To that extent, you will discard any label or stigma attached to your name and identity, and you will dispense with any wrong identity and wrong naming. Furthermore, you will seek and embrace that which is from God because it will define who you really are, what He created you to do and where He wants you to go.

In Biblical times, names were even more intentional than they are today, often saying something about that person's character or their calling. For example, David's name means beloved; he was known as a man who passionately pursued God's own heart. No matter what name you may be known by, even if God has not changed your name as He did with these Bible characters, nonetheless, you are called by His name by virtue of having surrendered your life to Him and become His own. As **Isaiah 43:1** says:

"But now, thus says the Lord, who created you, O Jacob, And He who formed you, O Israel: 'Fear not, for I have redeemed you; I have called you by your name; You are Mine'."

The Bible says that God knows us by name. He calls us by name in accordance with our purpose and destiny.

Sometimes, it becomes necessary to change your name once you come to the revelation about the power in a name and its impact on your destiny. A change suggests that you realize that the name up until now contradicts who and what you were born to be.

Names in the Bible can signify origin, recording some aspects of a person's birth.

Biblical names sometimes expressed the parents' reaction to the birth of their child (Hannah, for example).

Biblical names were sometimes used to secure the solidarity of family ties.

Names in the Bible can signify purpose.

Biblical names could be used to communicate God's message – for example, Immanuel, meaning "God with us."

Biblical names were also used to establish an affiliation with God.

For example, Isaiah ("God is Salvation"), Elijah *("Yahweh is God")*.

Biblical names were given to establish authority, or to indicate a new beginning or new direction in a person's life. As we have already seen, Abram's name was changed to Abraham to indicate that he was no longer childless but a father of many nations.

Names in the Bible honour God. Today, many parents give their child a name that honours God in some way. You may have planned to choose a name that honoured God all along, or you may have experienced difficulties in conceiving or during pregnancy that turned your eyes desperately or joyously upward. Hannah gave her child the name "Samuel" which means that "God heard."

In seeking to know your true identity;

- *You will need to master the passwords that open this truth to your soul.*
- *You will need to arrest the swindlers that steal your identity and lead you to an identity crisis.*
- *You will need to make daily confessions to keep reinforcing your identity.*
- *You will also need to identify the voices within you that shape you.*
- *You will need to recognize the paradoxes within and around you that give you that extra edge.*

Addressing these things is the beginning of discovering *the who you were born to be.*

- *You are unique.*
- *One of a kind.*
- *There is no one else quite like you.*
- *You have your own, special identity and you have your own unparalleled destiny.*
- *Your identity comprises certain traits and characteristics that distinguish you from everyone else.*
- *You are not a duplicate – a copy of another person.*
- *There is no one else on earth who can be the person that you are meant to be or do the work that you are called to do.*

Destiny Questions To Ponder On

1. *Are you the woman who does not know 'the who' she was born to be?*

2. *Are you the woman who rejects 'the who' she was born to be?*

3. *Are you the woman who is what others want her to be?*

4. *Are you the woman who allows circumstances, adversity and her past to say who she is?*

5. *Are you the woman who misrepresents who she should be to get ahead?*

6. *Are you the woman who allows her roles and other transient things to say who she is?*

7. *Are you the woman who allows her ego to say who she is?*

Chapter Two

THE PASSWORDS TO YOUR TRUE IDENTITY

Knowing What Should and What Should Not Define You

Chapter Preview

1. *Your Choices Define You*

2. *Your Purpose Defines You*

3. *Your Beliefs and Core Values Define You*

4. *Your Hallmarks Define You*

5. *Your Footprints Define You*

6. *Your Relationships Define You*

7. *Your Voice Defines You*

OPENING REMARKS

The Passwords to Your True Self-Identified

Passwords are keys and indicators that will lead you into unlocking and understanding what should and should not define you. These will include, your **choices** and decisions, your **Purpose** and Calling, your core-**values** that you have chosen to live by, your **hallmarks**, **characteristics** and trademarks that distinguish you, your **footprints** and legacy, your **relationships** and associations that you have chosen to be in and surround yourself with and your **voice** which represents your opinions and views on fundamental issues.

You are not defined by people's opinions, money, social status or success. Neither are you defined by your past pain, failures, weaknesses or roles. These things may shape and teach you valuable lessons but they do not define you because you are so much more than that.

1. YOUR CHOICES DEFINE YOU

"Our choices define and sculpture us" ~ **Sheena Hutchinson.**

Each and every one of us is who we are, where we are, doing what we are doing, and in the relationships that we are in, as a consequence of **choices** we have made, whether good or bad, whether these choices were made knowingly or unknowingly.

Your choices will affect the outcome of every area of your life, whether your health, your wealth, your relationships, your family, your career, your Calling, your walk with God, your role and position in society and in your nation etc.

"Choices are the hinges of Destiny." ~ **Edwin Markham**

One of the most powerful things you will possess in your life is the power of choice and since as an adult, no one can make your choices for you except yourself then it means that you must own those choices and their consequences whether good or bad.

"It is choice not chance that determines your Destiny" ~ **Jean Nidetch**

You are a sum total of the choices you select, because a choice is when you select between two or more options regarding anything that affects your life. Your choices will often be with regard to your relationships, your career, your health, your Destiny etc.

"Our lives are fashioned by our choices. First, we make our choices, then our choices make us." ~ **Anne Frank**

You either make a right choice, a wrong choice or no choice at all (abstain) meaning that failing to make a choice whether good or bad is a choice in itself.

"Your life is a product of your choices." ~ **Dr Kathleen Hall**

Factors that motivate your choices include; understanding what influences your choices e.g., past experiences, biases and prejudices, emotions, mind-set, beliefs, etc. will greatly assist you in weighing those choices so as to make the right ones.

"The decisions you make are a choice of values that reflect your life in every way." ~ **Alice Waters**

Our focus and actions also determine and cements our choices, so never make permanent decisions or choices based on a temporary situation.

When making conscious choices, the factors to include, identifying the problem that is requiring you to make a choice, gathering adequate and relevant information, examining the alternatives available, weighing the evidence available, and considering the consequences for each choice.

"The difference between an impulse and a conscious choice can mean failure or success" ~ **Unknown**

Your choices reflect your values, so review your decisions, take action, test your choices against your values, using your experience from lessons learnt in the past.

"It is not hard to make the right choices if you know what your values are." ~ **Roy E. Disney**

Your character and integrity are tested every time when you make a choice.

Your choices can either make you or break you, you are where you are today, doing what you are doing, and with who you are today, as a consequence of your choices.

"A highly proactive Woman will make conscious choices based on her principles and values rather than on feeling and conditions" ~ **Steven Covey**

In his book, *Seven Habits of a Highly Effective People,* renowned author, Steve Covey, explains "responsibility" as comprising of two words namely "response and 'ability' and he goes further to explain that while you have no choice in what happens to you, you have a choice in how to respond to it, whether appropriately or inappropriately, which in itself is a choice on your part.

When redeeming your wrong choices, it means that you must first acknowledge that you have made bad choices in order for you to rectify and redeem them, and thereafter, make new and right choices in order to change your life. The quality of your character and the strength of your inner spirit will enable you to survive bad choices.

"Do not be deceived, God is not mocked; for whatever a man sows that he will also reap." **(Galatians 6:7)**

Steve Covey goes further to say, *"Until you can say deeply and honestly, 'I am what I am today because of the choices I made yesterday', then you cannot say you choose otherwise."*

It simply takes a revoking and reversing of your early wrong decisions and making new right choices in order to get back on the right track. i.e., change your choices, change your life.

Your choices that you make every day will either move you closer or further away from your Destiny and your choices will lead you to either success or failure so your choices become your life.

"Your life is a sum of all your choices" ~ *Albert Camus*

Choices have consequences and the more fundamental the choice the greater the ramification and the more people affected by that choice.

"Every choice has an end result" ~ **Zig Ziglar**

Your choices today reflect who you are tomorrow, so you are free to make whatever choices you want but you are not free from the consequences of those choices.

"I believe that we are solely responsible for our choices, and we have to accept the consequences of every deed, word and thought throughout our lifetime." ~ **Elisabeth Kubler'rass**

2. YOUR PURPOSE DEFINES YOU

"Having a sense of Purpose is having a sense of self" ~ **Bryant H. McGill**

Purpose is basically "the why" you were created, that which you were specifically anointed and endowed for. Your Purpose consists of a series of assignments that you will fulfil towards your Destiny. Once you discover your Purpose and you begin to fulfil it successfully, that Purpose will be one of the passwords to your identity by which you will be defined.

Let us suppose that your Calling and Purpose is to be a minister of the gospel, a prophet or preacher or a political leader in a nation, such as a president, king or queen, or to be a leading business entrepreneur who builds national economies or, a writer/author, etc. then that call and Purpose does define you, to the extent that you do engage in fulfilling it and you become known for and identified with it. Hence it is important to discover your Purpose and fulfil it, because it is a password to your true identity.

The life Purpose you were created for is specific to you and you are uniquely endowed for it. God ordained your Purpose before he created you, so to that extent your identity is tied to your Purpose and therefore your Purpose defines your true identity. **Jeremiah 1:5** *"Before I formed you in the womb, I knew you; before you were born, I sanctified you; I ordained you a prophet to the nations."* This bible verse confirms that indeed your life Purpose and call defines who you are.

For example, in the bible, in the book Esther the young orphan Hadassah discovered **"the why" (Purpose)** she was in the king's palace in such a time and then she automatically understood **" the who" (identity)** she was born to be, namely as Queen Esther, a powerful intercessor and kingdom strategists who saved her people from annihilation. In other words, her Purpose defined her.

However, your Purpose and Call will only be effective in defining you if indeed you are successful in fulfilling it and its impact and positive influence becomes evident to those around you, in other words even if you have discovered your Purpose but you are not fulfilling it you cannot then expect to be defined by that Purpose.

3. YOUR BELIEFS AND CORE VALUES DEFINE YOU

"Your core-values are the deeply held beliefs that authentically describe your soul." ~ **John C. Maxwell**

Core values are principles or beliefs that you should view as being fundamental and of central importance to you and by which you choose to operate in all areas of your life as guiding lights in and out of season. Your core values are a password to your identity.

Your core-values may include; accountability, kindness, compassion, integrity, truthfulness, reliability, consistency, decency, justice and fairness etc. which people will define you by. Your values will guide your choices and behaviours and will set your principles and habits. Those values you live and walk by will definitely guide you in understanding and discovering who you are and your true identity.

Our values are often revealed in the way we choose to act and behave and what we give priority to because we will often back it up with actions and our actions reflect our values thereby defining us.

Our values are extensions of ourselves so they are what defines us because we are essentially what we value and our identity and self is the sum of everything we value. So, in seeking to find out who you are, you are in essence seeking the values that define you.

"Your values create your internal compass that can navigate how you make decisions in your life. If you compromise your values, you go nowhere" ~ **Roy T. Bennett**

4. YOUR HALLMARKS DEFINE YOU

Closely related to our core-values and beliefs are our hallmarks which depict our characteristics and our character and we know that a good character is shaped by our values and it is those values that enable us to distinguish between right and wrong, enabling us to make healthy and well-informed decisions and choices.

Your character and integrity are tested when you make a choice and your hallmarks are basically, your characteristics, your qualities, and your traits which become your trademarks by which you are known and identified. An inward character versus an external cosmetic appearance.

Your hallmark is your most distinctive typical quality or feature, your badge, your emblem, your trademark. A unique attribute like for example soft hearted and compassionate.

Some of the hallmarks of a serious Destiny Woman include being:

- **A game changer** – ability to change the game in every situation that you step into. A game changer means a identity that is able to contribute and affect a significant shift in the current way of doing or thinking about something so that in your Place of Assignment, you are a game changer in order to a make positive impact and influence. Being a game changer will entail you taking risks, facing opposition.

"Be a game changer the world has enough followers." ~ **Unknown**

- **A trail blazer** – the ability to make new tracks, inroads, impact and influence in areas, and sectors where others have not ventured before or others fear to venture. It is more or less ground breaking, spear heading, pioneering and trend setting and being a path finder.

"Don't be a spectator be a trailblazer." ~ **Unknown**

- **An influencer** – the ability to positively influence whoever and whatever you touch and wherever you trend positively with your passion, ideas, input, so as to leave those you touch positively transformed and the areas you trend on.

"To be an influencer, you have to love people before you can try to lead them." ~ **John C. Maxwell**

- **An authentic self**

"Authenticity is the daily practice of letting go of who we think we are supposed to be and embracing who we are." ~ **Brene Brown**

- This is the ability to be who you really are instead of being who others want you to be. Being authentic is risky because it means being open and vulnerable enough to be your true self and often this can lead to being hurt by others. Bishop T. D. Jakes is categorical in stating that you can never be effective unless you are truly authentic. *"Authenticity requires a certain measure of vulnerability, transparency and integrity."* ~ **Janet Louise Stephenson**

5. YOUR FOOTPRINTS DEFINE YOU

Your footprints that you will leave after fulfilling your Purpose definitely define you. **Footprints** means the impression left by a foot or shoe on the ground or a surface symbolizing the mark impact or benefit that fulfilling your Purpose will leave upon a generation, a society and a nation.

A living legend - the resolve to build a legacy by doing things extremely well and making your impact even while you are still alive. It shows your value and relevance to the society and nation. Long after you are gone, your legacy will only be stronger. Your legacy definitely defines you.

6. YOUR RELATIONSHIPS DEFINE YOU

"Surround yourself with like-minded, strong people, use your voices and choose courage over fear." ~ **Lilly Singh**

The company you keep does have an impact and influence on the choices you make and generally on your life and the people you associate with consistently and the causes you vocally affiliate and align yourself with will definitely define you. This is because associating, aligning and affiliation goes to the core of your beliefs and values and your beliefs and values definitely define you.

"Your associations are both subtle and powerful." ~ **Unknown**

The people and causes you associate with consistently either influence you positively or negatively, in fact the Bible says bad company corrupts good morals, and it is widely known that you are who you hang around with.

1 Cor 15:33 *"Do not be deceived: "Evil company corrupts good habits."*

Your associations include your networks whether in business, in your profession and in your social life which will end up defining you as, if you continue to associate with them consistently whether openly and publicly or privately.

"Associate yourself with people of good quality, for it is better to be alone than in bad company." ~ **Booker J. Washington**

Your interest groups such as club memberships, political groups, SACCOs and *chamas* etc. that you are a member of, will usually have Vision and mission statements and core values which you are deemed to have embraced by virtue of your membership and association in and with them. So, your associations are a pointer to what you enjoy doing and who you enjoy doing it with, and are therefore also a pointer to what kind of people and activities you place value on. You are the average of the five people you spend most of your time with.

7. YOUR VOICE DEFINES YOU

"When the whole world is silent, even one voice becomes powerful." ~ **Malala Yousafzai**

In this context your voice symbolizes your views, opinions and what you stand for which you express articulately, strongly, passionately and consistently especially publicly.

Your voice is either that which you stand for, believe in etc. whether expressly or implied or that which you speak up for verbally or by your silence.

"Words mean more than what is set down on paper. It takes the human voice to infuse them with deeper meaning." ~ **Maya Angelou**

Your words are powerful and they add power to your voice, and to that extent, words that you speak regarding fundamental life issues have the effect of binding you and becoming an intrinsic part of you and thereby define who you are. For example, when you use your words to confess that Jesus is Lord and Savior you are defined by that confession and it becomes part of your identity.

- Your views and opinions that you make known publicly and you are known for regarding various fundamental issues that affect society e.g., politics, race, religion, ethnicity, wealth etc. Defines you.
- Your self-expressions, are also your voice for example in how you use of your wealth, resources, time, energy, your creativity, namely where do you most invest yourself in, is it entertainment, education, business, spiritual, financial etc.
- Also, the things you have mastered and your area of mastery and outstanding expertise, where you are an authoritative source.
- Your voice also includes your microphone, platform, your designated space, social media, TV, radio, books and magazines etc. are all symbols of your voice that defines who you are, by what you strongly believe.
- Your voice also includes your vote, because it expresses your preferences which are based on your values and if your values define you then your vote surely defines you.

"Don't let the noise of other's opinions drown out your own inner voice." ~ **Steve Jobs**

Your voice may also be strongest and loudest in your silence because as a leading Woman in your society and nation when you are silent on fundamental issues which people expect you to have an opinion on then your silence can speak volumes. Knowing that your voice defines you therefore begs that you be very cautious about how you use that voice.

"Listen to your own voice, your own soul. Too many people listen to the noise of the world, instead of themselves." ~ **Leon Brown.**

In conclusion, as you use these passwords to unlock your true identity and establish you in a strong and secure sense of self, you must put away anything transient that you have allowed to define you plus every negative narrative, stigmas and labels that have plagued you and hindered and held back your true identity and effectiveness. Stand on a new reality of truth as to **"the who"** you were born to be.

Destiny Questions to Ponder On

1. *What fundamental* **choices** *have you made in your life that you feel have defined you? Either positively or negatively.*

2. *To what extent do you believe that your* **Purpose** *has defined you?*

3. *Which of your many* **core values** *do you believe defines you most?*

4. *What 3* **hallmarks** *do you believe people associate you with most?*

5. *What* **footprints** *have you left and where?*

6. *Are there* **relationships** *currently in your life that you believe define you in a way you rather not to be defined?*

7. *Which aspect of* **"voice"** *do you believe defines you most accurately?*

This Page Was Intentionally Left Blank

Chapter Three

THE TRIGGERS TO AN IDENTITY CRISIS

Arresting Your Identity Thieves

Chapter Preview

OPENING REMARKS

Equally important to finding the passwords that will unlock your true identity is discerning the several factors that will steal your identity and throw you into an identity crisis.

"No death, no doom, no anguish that can arouse the surpassing despair which flows from a loss of identity." ~ **H.P. Lovecraft**

When you begin to question who you are, and it begins to affect your daily thinking or functioning, then you are suffering from an identity crisis, which becomes a serious threat to your identity.

Some of the most common threats to your identity that lead to an identity crisis include, dwelling on your past pain, frustrations from failing constantly, the poisonous effect of people's opinions, inability to discover and embark on your Purpose, confusion about your roles in the various areas of your life, the scars of painful traumatic events, and when you remain in a place of cluttered-ness etc.

It is a season of uncertainty and confusion in which your sense of identity becomes insecure due to those and other several factors.

The symptoms may include questioning who you are, overall or with regard to certain aspects of your life like age, career, relationships etc. which may lead to a conflict and inner turmoil.

Considering how crucial a secure identity is in fulfilling your Purpose and attaining your Destiny, it becomes imperative that you remain aware of any symptoms of an identity crisis and seek to address them at your earliest, to avoid derailing your Destiny.

Identifying the identity thieves, arresting them will secure and keep your identity intact.

"But as many as received Him, to them He gave the right to become children of God, to those who believe in His name." **John. 1:12**

1. THE PRISON OF PAST PAIN

One of the things that distort our self–identity or our security in our identity is past painful experiences that plague and paralyze us from moving forward. You must acknowledge your past pain then you must purposefully and intentionally open yourself up to confronting and overcoming it and embrace the healing process.

"Never let the pain from your past punish your present and paralyze your future." ~ **Unknown**

When your chronic pain is no longer useful as a symptom towards treatment then your identity is challenged and weakened.

Beware of the effects of chronic physical pain from sickness and infirmity toxic emotions from your past pain such as offence, bitterness, resentment, anger, unforgiving because they steal your identity.

Every one of us has been hurt but it is what you do with that hurt that is more important than the hurt and your ability to learn from your past and let it become nuggets of wisdom

"The past is a waste paper and the present is a newspaper and the future is a question paper so come out of your past, control the present and secure your future." **Unknown**

Past pain causes us to forget who we are, because the pain blinds us and deafens us until we do not know where we are coming from or where we are going. Let your today's joys, heal the sting of yesterday's pain. Stop questioning your value because of your incapacity and loss. Make a conscious decision to let go of the past, Purpose to move on no matter how clumsily, but move on, it is a process not an overnight healing.

Restoring your security in your identity will require you to heal from past pain and wounded-ness and stop allowing your hurt feelings to override everything else until nothing else matters stop empowering those who hurt you by continuing in your pain. Forgiveness is not weakness it sets you free.

"Forget all the pains of the past, they were meant to make you stronger. Start walking towards the future and blame no one as wrong." ~ **Unknown**

Do not allow past pain to define, destroy, defeat and deter you, but allow it to strengthen you and do not get *stuck* in your pain and stubbornness, forgiveness is for yourself more than for others so forgive and refuse that victim mentality and blame shifting.

Chronic physical pain arising out of chronic sickness that has been prolonged can steal your self-identity like the Woman in the bible with the issue of blood because beyond the physical pain is the pain of delayed or lost dreams or goals and the pain that you may never fulfil your Purpose and Destiny. So, it is therefore important to address and manage chronic pain and more importantly to restructure your dreams, goals and plans in a way that you will still fulfil your Purpose and Destiny, despite any infirmity or physical incapacity.

Learn to focus on the present moments develop positive self-affirmation, declarations and decrees and daily positive confessions, to encourage and edify yourself.

In summary, you must ensure that your pain whether past or present, physical or emotional does not steal your self-identity and delay and hinder your Purpose and Destiny.

2. THE FRUSTRATION OF CHRONIC FAILURES

"Failure is simply the opportunity to begin again" ~ **Henry Ford**

Failure means a lack of success, the non-fulfillment of a desired goal or goals, defeat, abortion and miscarriage of Purpose, inability to perform or complete something successfully.

Generally, failure is caused by fear of failure itself, lack of persistence, lack of focus or discipline, fatalistic attitudes, wrong and negative confessions, and a lack of conviction etc. The general consequences of failure are basically feeling demoralized, discouraged and depressed.

You may have experienced these frustrations of failure in either one of the following areas of your life which has seriously shaken and eroded your self-identity.

- **In Your Relationships** *(Relationship failure)*

This may include broken engagements to marry, a failed marriage or broken business, relationship, professional relationships and even broken spiritual relationships with your spiritual leaders or your brethren.

Failure in your relationships can affect your self-identity especially where you may think you are responsible for the failure and even where you may not feel responsible for the failure, the rejection and abandonment may shake your identity.

- **In Your Parenting** *(Parenting Failure)*

Where children go astray and you blame yourself because you feel you neglected them at crucial seasons in their lives and sensitive ages in their lives and you now regret that they did not turn out the way they should have and you attribute that to your failed parenting skills.

- **In Your Finances and Businesses** *(Financial failure)*

You may make bad investments and incur losses which may or may not end up in bankruptcy and at the very least financial disorientation and devastation.

- **In Your Profession and Career** *(Career failure)*

This is where you regret missed opportunities, made wrong connections and choices etc. which led you to fail in your career and profession and you have nothing to show for it or what you have is very little. This could also mean feeling seriously delayed in getting to where you thought you would be and feeling that you are way behind your peers in terms of achievements.

- **In Your Moral Judgments** *(Moral Failure)*

This is where you have made unfortunate errors in your choices and judgment leading to moral failures, unethical dealings and scandals that have tainted your reputation either in business, in the profession and socially. This kind of failure can leave you feeling unworthy and strip you off your identity.

- **In Your Calling and Purpose** *(Abortion of Purpose)*

Where you know what your Calling and Purpose is, but for whatever reasons you haven't made any progress in fulfilling it for example as an artist, politician, leader, preacher etc. and the regret can lead to the fear of failing again which can often paralyze us from moving forward thereby keeping us in a state of stagnation, which causes us to lose confidence in our identity and in our abilities.

- **In Your Spiritual Walk With God** *(Backsliding)*

Perhaps you are a shepherd or a church leader who is caught and exposed in a scandal etc. or a **saint** who walks away from the faith. This is where you might have backslidden and turned away from God and the things of God and this can seriously affect your self–identity where previously you were identified as a child of God who has now strayed away.

All these are thieves that seek to swindle you of your identity and you must acknowledge, confront and overcome them for the sake of your Purpose and Destiny.

THE POISON OF PEOPLE'S OPINIONS

"You will not be criticized by someone who is doing more than you, you will be criticized by someone who cannot do more than you, remember that!" ~ **Unknown**

What people say and what they do not say, how they look at you, how they judge and view you can be poisonous.

Failure to define yourself will always lead to other people defining you and stigmatizing you with negative and limiting labels to suit their Purposes.

"Stop allowing other people to dilute or poison your day with their words or opinion. Stand strong in the truth of your beauty and journey through your day without attachment to the validation of others." ~ **Steven Maraboli**

One cannot define someone or something they did not create or manufacture and since you were not created by other people, they have no right to define you and you must therefore reject their misguided label of you.

Different people will define you differently because they are using their own projections which will throw you into confusion until you have no idea of who you are.

You are not other people's opinion. Beware of making radical shifts in your views and opinions to suit other people. Form your own opinions and views about yourself and do not empower other people by adjusting to their opinions of you.

Being desperate for people's approval and seeking to conform to meet other people's expectations and being a people pleaser is a tragic attempt to seek your value through other people's approval.

Beware of co-dependency —which is characterized by a dysfunctional, one -sided relationship where one relies on the other for meeting nearly all of their emotional and self-esteem needs. It also describes a relationship that **encourages** one to maintain their irresponsible, addictive, or underachieving behaviour, because you allow them to whether knowingly or unknowingly.

"It is not what they call you, it's what you answer to. Don't let the noise of other people's opinions draw out and silence your voice." ~ **An African proverb.**

Do not allow the poisonous people opinions steal your identity.

THE LETHARGIC LACK OF PURPOSE

"The soul without a fixed Purpose is lost"

Just like discovering your Purpose walking in it and fulfilling it defines you, likewise **NOT** knowing your Purpose nor walking in it and fulfilling it will lead you into an identity crisis, failure to have a revelation as to "the what" you were created to do will lead you to lacking a Purpose which erodes your identity.

Failure to consult and seek wise counsel from mentors and spiritual midwives as to how to discover your Purpose, will leave you with a lack of Purpose and being distracted and focusing on activities that do not add value to your life will deny you the time to discover your real Purpose and without a Purpose, your true identity becomes suspect.

Being self-absorbed and self-centred and selfish and remaining in a comfort zone of only what pleases and benefits you will leave you with a lack of Purpose associating and surrounding yourself with people without Purpose will also leave you with a lack of Purpose.

"A self-identity without a Purpose is like a ship without a rudder."
Thomas Carlyle

Lack of Purpose therefore will steal your self-identity and you must therefore seek that Purpose because it defines who you are.

THE TURMOIL OF A ROLE CRISIS

"Every role that you play comes with its own set of challenges." ~
Mireille Enos

Your role is a function, a position or title which includes duties and responsibilities and mandates whether in a family, an organization or in a business, ministry etc. even though your various roles in life do not define you, nonetheless the challenges they come with can overwhelm you and encroach on your self-identity.

"Success in one role can't justify failure in another." ~ **Stephen Covey**

There are different reasons why you can encounter **"a role failure"** leading you into **"role confusion"** and thereby affecting your identity e.g., where your **"role is random"** and unclear so that even you are unable to specify what your role is.

Where your role keeps changing erratically without giving you enough time to exit your old role, prepare for the new role emotionally or where there is a **"reversal of roles"** like gender roles where a husband plays the role of a wife and vice versa or a child plays the role of a parent.

In other instances, it is where you have a **"role exit"** by abandoning and changing from one profession to another, or where you have **overlapping and multiple roles**, they can become overwhelming and stressful leading to a **"role conflict"** and **"role strain."**

Where any of the above happens with regard to your role either in a society or in an organization or in a family, then you may encounter an identity crisis.

Therefore, you must learn to recognize these occurrences, address and manage them, before they erode your identity.

THE AGONY OF TRAUMATIC TRENDS

"Trauma is a fact of life. It does not however have to be a life sentence" ~ *Peter A. Levine*

Perhaps you have suffered traumatic events that left you numb, keeping you bound and stagnant, unable to continue fulfilling your Purpose and Destiny.

Trauma is damage to the mind caused by distressing events. It can also be relentless and excessive stress that is beyond your capacity to cope with and trauma can either be from one isolated event or from a series of recurring events and it can come as a result of separation, abandonment, abuse, assaults, attacks and accidents etc.

Trauma causes fear, shock, soul wounds, confusion, mood swings, nightmares and even insomnia all in great intensity and degree.

Trauma affects your **self-identity** because it affects your perception and also impacts on your self-identity by affecting your relationship with yourself and with others by shattering your ability to be in control of your life and your ability to make sound choices and decisions.

It erodes your self-esteem and confidence when you feel incapable and weak leading to self-hate, shame and guilt which then erodes your self-identity.

Death and loss of a loved one may traumatically erode your identity and it can totally devastate you and throw you into a place of such darkness that you forget who you are or where you are going. However, you must purpose to climb out of that darkness for the sake of fulfilling your Destiny.

"There are wounds that never show on the body that are deeper and more hurtful than anything that bleeds." ~ **Laurell K. Hamilton**

Another type of trauma that can violently shake your identity is *Rejection and abandonment* which can lead you into an identity crisis because of the sense of worthlessness that it brings upon you.

You must Purpose to heal from all these traumas through all the support systems and mechanisms available so that you arise and move on to your Destiny.

"The paradox of trauma is that it has both the power to transform and resurrect" ~ **Peter A. Levine**

Reclaim your identity by allowing the grieving period and process, join trauma survivor groups and do not isolate yourself. This is of course easier said than done, but remember that nothing no matter how devastating is ever intended to destroy you because your Purpose and Destiny will always preserve you, let your passion for your Purpose and Destiny be the greatest motivation for wanting to heal from these traumatic trends because where there is a will, there is a way.

THE CHAOS OF A CLUTTERED LIFESTYLE

"Beware of the barrenness of an overcrowded life" ~ **Unknown**

Cluttered-ness can be so subtle that it may take you a long time to realize that you are cluttered in one area of your life or another.

Emotional cluttered-ness is when you harbour past pain, woundedness, bitterness, unforgiving, offense, frustration, disappointments, hatefulness, guilt and you become so emotionally cluttered that you are unable to make room for anything good and you hinder any healthy and credible identity. You should address these emotions as opposed to denying them and then forgive and be detoxed of them.

"Clutter steals energy and joy." **Monika Kristofferson**

Spiritual cluttered-ness is when you are confused about who and what you believe in or when you mix yourself up with so many different doctrines or you drink from contaminated spiritual wells and you surround yourself with strange fires and carry strange burdens. You become so cluttered that it is difficult to have an identity as to who you are in the true God. You should ensure that you are worshipping at a bible believing church at the right altar, listening to the correct doctrine and having a relationship with Christ as opposed to practicing empty religion or being bound by cults and idolatry.

"Hold fast the pattern of sound words which you have heard from me, in faith and love which are in Christ Jesus" **(2 Timothy 1:13)**

Mental cluttered-ness is when you are unable to sieve your thoughts or to pull down strongholds in your mind and when your mind is congested with lofty imaginations, untruths and distorted truth then you become too cluttered to know who you are. You should control the thoughts that you allow into your mind, adopt a positive not a negative mind-set, watch what you read and watch and feed on the pure, true and noble.

"Finally, brethren, whatever things are true, whatever things are noble, whatever things are just, whatever things are pure, whatever things are lovely whatever things are of good report, if there is any virtue and if there is anything praiseworthy, meditate on these things." **(Philippians 4:8)**

Financial cluttered-ness is your inability to manage your finances and resources and your inability to have a healthy relationship with your money, and your misconceptions as to the place of money in your life and your inability to master your money and instead you allow your money to master you and thereby being obsessed with greed for mammon will leave you cluttered and wondering what really defines you. You should plan, budget, discern and address your money language.

"NO one can serve two masters; for either he will hate the one and love the other, or else he will be loyal to the one and despise the other. You cannot serve God and mammon" **(Matthew 6:24)**

Social cluttered-ness is when you have too many relationships and activities which are not all necessary because you are not intended to relate to everybody in the world and your inability to sieve and sift your relationships, your social activities, your social networks will leave you so cluttered that you have no clear identity. You should filter, sieve, select and discriminate your social life. Carry your own monkeys, fight your own battles. Develop and maintain healthy Destiny relationships and activities. Choose carefully who you give access to your life.

Intellectual cluttered-ness is your inability to sieve and sift the information and knowledge that you will feed on so you end up taking in everything from everywhere whether useful for your Purpose or not will leave you cluttered and without a clear identity. You should distinguish between what you need for your Destiny and what you don't, because not everything is profitable.

"All things are lawful for me, but not all things are helpful; all things are lawful for me, but not all things edify." **(1 Cor. 10:23)**

"All things are lawful for me, but all things are not helpful. All things are lawful for me, but I will not be brought under the power of any." **(1Cor. 6:12)**

Physical cluttered-ness is this is when you have amassed and accumulated so much unnecessary junk in your physical spaces. When you fail to declutter your physical space, it is a reflection of the cluttered-ness of your mental and emotional state and it may affect your self-identity.

"A cluttered house is a cluttered mind." **Unknown**

Some homes and houses are so cluttered they lose their beauty. Your inability to let go items in your wardrobe or any part of your home maybe a sign of deeper issues within you like a "hoarding" condition. Open your heart and give away as much as possible of what you know you don't need or use whether it is clothes, kitchenware, furniture etc. As Oprah Winfrey says very often if you have outfits in your wardrobe, you have not worn for like 6 months, they should leave your wardrobe.

Take steps and action to get rid of all clutter in your life; through deliberate steps and action and protect your identity from becoming an identity crisis.

"Out of clutter find simplicity." **Albert Eisten**

Destiny Questions to Ponder On

1. Can you put your finger on a specific **pain** in your life that threatens your identity, whether it be physical, emotional, mental, financial, social, spiritual etc.?

2. How have you responded and dealt with **failures** in your life that have threatened your identity?

3. How do you differentiate between people's positive views and people's poisonous opinions?

4. Do you believe that one's failure or delay to discover their **Purpose** affects their identity?

5. Which one aspect of your **roles** do you believe poses the most danger to your identity, is it a role exit, role failure, random rules, overlapping roles or multiple roles etc.?

6. Have you ever experienced a **trauma** that eroded your identity and if so, how did you restore your self-identity?

7. Which aspects of your life do you consider **most cluttered**, is it emotionally, mentally, physically, financially, socially, spiritually, occupationally/ vocationally etc. and in which ways has that damaged your identity?

This Page Was Intentionally Left Blank

Chapter Four

THE VOICES THAT SHAPE YOU

Sieving Who and What You Hear

Chapter Preview

1. *The Voice of a Parent*
2. *The Voice of Mentors and Role Models*
3. *The Voice of Friends*
4. *The Voices of the Past*
5. *Your Inner Voice*
6. *The Voice of Destiny*
7. *The Voice of God*

OPENING REMARKS

"I think we all have a little voice inside us that will guide us. It may be God, I don't know but I think if we shut out all the noise and clutter from our lives and listen to that voice, it will tell us the right thing to do." **~ Christopher Reeves.**

Within everyone no matter how stable and well put together you are, there are different voices within and around you seeking and competing to define you. It will be up to you to decide which voices you will allow yourself to listen to and which voices you will silence.

"The more you listen to your inner voice, the quieter you will get." **~ Unknown**

In your journey to Destiny, you will encounter many cross roads at which point you must arise and make crucial Destiny decisions, based on the voices you have allowed to influence you.

Everyone in today's world will identify with one or several stories, scenarios and illustrations whether in their career, Calling, business, family or spiritual life etc. and the question is what predominant voice within and around you carries the day.

In any situation, the key that unlocks the right Destiny decision is dependent on the voices that each one chooses to listen to and the voices they chose to silence.

"Who you listen to is who you follow and who you follow determines major decisions in your life." **~ Unknown**

As stated, there will be several and different voices that will seek to compete for your attention at every turn in your journey to

Destiny such as the victim's voice versus the victor's voice, the voice of doubt versus the voice of faith, the voice of fear versus the voice of courage, the voice of past pain and failure versus the voice of health and wellness etc.

"It is easy to get distracted by dissenting voices and naysayers, even if it's one. But don't let it affect you. Don't let it influence you. Think of the majority who appreciate what you do. That should keep you going. Besides, your reward is with the Almighty. Not humankind." ~ **Mufti Ismail Menk**

You are the voices you listen to and the advice you follow so that the voices within you or around you whether yours or influenced by others will often shape your clarity and reality.

"The voice you believe will determine your Destiny, God's truth or the devils lie." ~ **Unknown**

Beware which voices you are allowing yourself to listen to because the voices you pay attention to can unleash or limit your potential and your possibilities and heeding wrong voices can cost you dearly in terms of Destiny.

"Don't let the noise of others opinion drown out your own inner voice" ~ **Steve Jobs**

It is true that you cannot erase how other people's voices have influenced your own voices but you have the choice to decide whether to listen to them or not.

It is very common and natural for us to be influenced by voices of people who we deem credible or knowledgeable, or the voices of people we love and trust or even voices of people we feel we owe for one reason or another.

Suffice to say that, when it comes to our Destiny, wisdom would surely suggest that we listen to the voice of God, he who has called us into that Destiny and the voices of those he has assigned to be our Destiny helpers etc. as well as our own inner voice that aligns with his word and his will for us.

1. THE VOICE OF A PARENT

"The way we talk to our children becomes their inner voice." **By Peggy O'mara**

The voice of a parent can either be verbal or non-verbal. The voice of a parent has a way of shaping your life regardless of your age, it can shape your concept of self, it can shape your perception, view on life, your beliefs, how you view others etc. and generally who you end up becoming. A parent's voice is the first voice a child hears so it is extremely significant in shaping you.

The non-verbal actions of a parent often speak louder than words and most of us were influenced by those non-verbal actions from a very early age and throughout our lives. Parents also have a tendency to use their eyes and body language to speak to us and that can communicate volumes.

In other words, a parent's voice whether verbal, non-verbal, through body language, actions or a look with their eyes can build or destroy your self-image, esteem, worth and value or it can do the exact opposite towards affirming, edifying and building your self-image, esteem and value.

As we grow older and become independent and begin to master our own Destinies, we must learn to differentiate between the aspects of our parent's voices that is negative and that which is positive and learn to choose the voice in them that we will allow to influence us. We must be selective on what we allow into our hearts.

2. THE VOICE OF MENTORS AND ROLE MODELS

"The influence of a good teacher can never be erased." **By Unknown**

These include teachers, coaches, pastors, primary caregivers, older siblings, influential employers, leaders, authority figures etc., who have impacted our lives greatly over the years and their voice has the capacity to either broaden our minds or block our minds. They can either instill an inferiority complex or a healthy complex.

Some can inspire, awaken curiosity, provoke, influence us positively, unleash our hidden potential etc. and some can do the exact opposite.

It is crucial that you learn to discern the voice from such people that will add you confidence and courage as opposed to fear and self-doubt. The right voice is the one that equips and empowers you towards your Destiny.

3. THE VOICE OF FRIENDS

"As much as people refuse to believe it, the company you keep does have an impact and influence on your choices." **By Unknown**

Friend's voice can affect the ways that you think and feel about yourself. How your friends think about and respond to you will, over time, have a strong influence on your perceptions of yourself. How you respond to situations in life and how you treat others as well.

The voice of a friend whether verbal or non -verbal can also influence each other's personal preferences and lifestyles.

The impact of the voices of your friends can influence a strong social network which is associated with a healthier and longer life.

Friends whose voices influence you on the negative either through wrong choices such as indulgence in conducts that jeopardize your career, family life and relations are to be avoided.

The voice of a friend who provokes, motivates and pushes you toward your Destiny is the voice you need to allow to shape you.

4. THE VOICES OF THE PAST

"Let go of the past, but keep the lesson it taught you" **By Chiara Gizzi**

The voices of past experiences can affect your cognition which is thoughts, ideas, beliefs, etc. The voice from your past has a way of influencing how you feel and think about current situations which in turn can affect your behaviour and action.

The voices from your past can be used positively to impact your decision making, as regards the type of people you choose to allow in your inner circle, the type of investments you will venture into etc.

Learning to sieve through which voice in your past you should listen to is very crucial. Past failures should inspire you to learn from the mistakes and rise up and use a different strategy to handle problems in the future when past strategies failed.

The voices of the past can impact your actions and how you deal with future challenges. ~ **Brandon Thomas, 2008**

You should be able to choose the voices of your past that inspire your future, by being more futuristic oriented than the past-oriented. This will drive you past disappointments, frustrations, failures and lead you to the place of planning ahead of time on how to handle future challenges. For example, where you experienced financial challenges in the past, then in the future you learn to budget ahead of time and avoid over expenditure on things that will deter your dreams and goals.

The voices of the past especially when you experienced challenges that were beyond your control, can be limiting if you choose to perceive things in a negative way.

Past failures can be paralyzing if you let it define you. Allowing issues of the past to give you an identity can often cripple your goals and stop your Destiny.

Looking back and allowing the voices of your past in to negatively dictate your decisions, directions and allowing fear to creep in can lead to termination of future successes, opportunities and forging forward towards your Destiny.

"It's is not the future that you are afraid of, it is repeating the past that makes you anxious." **By Unknown**

5. YOUR INNER VOICE

"Always listen to your inner voice." **By Oprah Winfrey**

It is important to differentiate between your inner voice that is **positive** and healthy which we normally refer to as your intuition, conscience and your instincts from your inner voice that is **negative** because it is usually an inner critic that is constantly demeaning and judging you.

Your inner voice consists of your ability to trust your gut, as someone may call it, on your conscious, to follow your intuition, and trust your instincts. Learning to decipher the voices in your head will enable you to listen to your positive inner voice.

Being able to identify between the voice of fear and your intuition, conscience and instincts can be beneficial in reclaiming your power and taking control of your life.

When things aren't in alignment with who you are or where you want to go, your inner knowing will alert you. Call it instinct, intuition or a gut feeling, conscious – there is something within you that tells you when following a certain path isn't right for you.

"Listen to your inner voice. Trust your intuition. It's important to have the courage to trust yourself." — **Dawn Ostroff**

Your inner voice asks you if you're certain making that decision is in your best interest. It questions whether or not you have enough information to make a decision. It asks you why you care and why this is important to you.

These inner voices usually come from early life experiences that are internalized and taken in as ways you think about yourself. On the other hand, the negative inner voices may come from your parents or primary care takers. As a child you may have picked up on the negative attitudes that parents not only had towards you but also toward themselves. Your voices can also come from interactions with peers and siblings, or influential adults.

People with a strong inner critic tend to have one thing in common namely however great their success, they don't feel it's genuine. *"The inner critic won't let them see their past achievements as 'real'"*. So, they may push themselves more, with diminishing returns, driven more by fear of failure than inspiration. (Pincott, 2019).

"Your inner voice is subtle but it grows stronger when you listen." **By Van Praach**

Fear and self-doubt are the worst enemies of your inner voice. Learning to differentiate whether fear is stopping you or just a caution of impending danger is of importance.

Overly criticizing yourself based on past failures is an inner giant you must slay, by being courageous and aggressive when facing unfamiliar grounds, which will help you overcome negative inner limiting voices.

In order to take power over any destructive thought process, you must first become conscious of what your inner voice is telling you, so you can stop it from ruining your life.

To identify this, it is helpful to pay attention, when you suddenly slip into a bad mood or become upset, often these negative shifts in emotion are a result of a critical inner voice.

Once you identify the thought process and pinpoint the negative actions it is advocating, you can take control over your inner voice by consciously deciding not to listen. Instead, you can take the actions that are in your best interest. (Badenoch, 2010)

The solution isn't to shut down the critic inner voice because that won't work and the voice will return no matter how hard you try to suppress it. Nor is it always effective to analyze the emotions it rouses because that opens you to the risk of ruminating or reliving those feelings and getting stuck in a negative cycle.

The best intervention may be to respond to its grievances from a detached perspective—almost as if you were another person, namely self-distancing which allows you to pause, step back and think clearly and rationally.

Self-affirmation has also proven to be a useful offset to self-criticism. When you hear a voice saying you're inferior or deficient, because affirmations can revise the negative messages you hear—or think you hear—from the voices of parental figures who were unable to show that they believed in you enough, or from a naturally neurotic or self-doubting personality.

You can help your self-compassion find its voice. You are encouraged to remember when your inner critic was born, so that you can give your younger self more sympathy and security than you received in the first go-round because ideally, a self-compassionate response emerges from healthy interaction and can, going forward, be called on as a buffer against self-criticism.

6. THE VOICE OF DESTINY

"Every man has his own destiny: the only imperative is to follow it, to accept it, no matter where it leads him." ~ **Henry Miller**

"Control your own destiny or someone else will." ~ **Jack Welch**

What are the voices you have heard during your life? Whether you know it or not, you have been programmed by the many voices you have heard. If you are not living the life you desire, you need to be re-programmed by the voice of your destiny.

Your voice of Destiny is that voice that pushes you towards what you were created for and the purpose to which you exist. When you choose to listen to the voice of Destiny you will strive for achievement, because the voice of your Destiny is calling you tend to work hard to develop your knowledge, skills and abilities.

The voice of your Destiny will cause you to pay attention to information that you can use to create positive outcomes in the future, engage in activities that will improve your situation. The voice of your Destiny will cause you to be inquisitive and try to figure out why things turned out the way they did, and to have a more participative and proactive role in your life and your Destiny (Claire Newton, 2020).

"To transform yourself is to transform your Destiny." **– Laura Esquivel**

The voice of Destiny will provoke you to know and own your identity, discover and fulfil your Purpose and Calling, locate and position yourself in your place and sphere of influence, identify and connect yourself to the people of your Destiny, embrace the process of your making and moulding, set and establish the principles and values that you will need and use to fulfil your purpose and Destiny, become empowered and equipped to lay hold of the rewards and prize that await you as you faithfully fulfil your Destiny.

"The best years of your life are the ones in which you decide your problems are your own. You do not blame them on your mother, the ecology, or the president. You realize that you control your own destiny." **– Albert Ellis**

7. THE VOICE OF GOD

"Don't let the voices of the world keep you from hearing the voice of God." **By Unknown**

God's voice is the main voice that you ought to listen to and allow to influence you.

God speaks all the time and everything He speaks is beneficial to you and your Destiny. Learning to tune into God's voice and learning to distinguish it from other voices will be important as you fulfil your Destiny.

"We often miss hearing God's voice simply because we aren't paying attention." **By Rick Warren**

Be constantly expectant to hear God's voice and be confident that you do hear His voice because His sheep hear his voice and you are His sheep.

God's voice is a still small voice that is distinct and cannot be ignored because God speaks through His spirit and you must constantly surrender yourself to the leading of the Holy Spirit. Spending time with God is the best way to learn how to hear Him.

God speaks His word; He never contradicts it. So, if what you think you have heard from God contradicts what His Word says then it is not the Voice of God that you heard.

"If you do all the talking when you pray, how will you ever hear God's answers?" **By Aiden Wilson Tozer**

Learning to discern the voice of God from your voice, the devil's voice and people's around you will help you hear God clearly. The voices of fear, unbelief and doubt are often the greatest enemies of your hearing God. Learning to meditate on the word of God, studying the word so as not to be swayed away from the truth and this will enable you align His voice with His word.

Learning to walk by faith and not by sight is often what we require when it comes to hearing the voice of God and walking in obedience to God's voice will help you grow in hearing Him as you continue to abide in Him.

"When you take time with God and listen to His voice, He renews your strength and enables you to handle life." **By Joyce Meyer**

Destiny Questions to Ponder on

1. *What aspects of your parents' voice do you feel has been positive in shaping you and what aspects do you feel have been negative in shaping you?*

2. *How have the voices of your mentors and role models shaped you this far?*

3. *Which voices of your friends have you had to silence over the years?*

4. *What is your greatest challenge in silencing negative voices of your past?*

5. *Do you believe that you have been able to distinguish between the positive aspect of your inner voice and the negative aspect of your inner voice?*

6. *Which particular voice of Destiny has empowered and equipped you most?*

7. *What hinders you from hearing the voice of God clearly?*

This Page Was Intentionally Left Blank

Chapter Five

THE DESTINY QUEEN OR THE DESTINY QUITTER

Owning and Wearing Your Crown for Destiny

Chapter Preview

1. *The Voice of a Winner or the Voice of a Loser.*

2. *The Voice of Your Destiny Helpers or the Voice of Your Destiny Killers.*

3. *The Voice of a Radical Game Changer or the Voice of a Lazy Lethargic.*

4. *The Voice of self-sacrifice or the Voice of Self-preservation.*

5. *The Voice from the Courage Zone or the Voice from the Comfort Zone.*

6. *The Voice that Votes to Fulfil Destiny or the Voice that Votes to Abort Destiny.*

7. *The Voice of a Victor or the Voice of a Victim.*

OPENING REMARKS

"People in positions of power and privilege have a duty to perform at a higher level. If not them then who?" ~ **Kathleen Parker**

As a Woman of Destiny, you may find yourself "crowned" and called to hold very powerful and privileged positions (either in your family, church, organization, business enterprise, Government, society or nation). Serious dilemmas, threats or crisis may arise and you must decide how to use those powerful privileged positions in resolving those dilemmas, averting those threats and crisis for the sake of the people, organizations, societies or nations that you have been crowned and called to protect and impact positively.

The voices within and around you will play a crucial role in either empowering or disempowering you to do the right thing.

These kinds of scenarios will require you to decide between accepting the responsibility that comes with that power and privilege or to abdicate or abscond from that responsibility.

A crown symbolizes power, privilege, authority, honour, glory and legitimacy and a real crown is very heavy which means that you cannot afford to look down once you have been crowned otherwise you will break your neck which symbolizes your confidence, courage and strength.

Consequently, your head must be constantly held up high in confidence and courage in order to rule and command your Place of Assignment and become a **Destiny Queen** as opposed to becoming a **Destiny Quitter** by virtue of having broken your neck, because you looked down in fear and doubt.

"Don't be afraid to wear your crown you're a queen, you're a king inside and outside." **~ Britt Nicole**

Your ability to wear your crown and hold your head up high will be determined by the voices within and around you that you have allowed to influence you.

"Your crown has been bought and paid for, put it on your head and wear it." **~ Maya Angelou**

A **Destiny Queen** is one who can bear the weight of her crown, symbolizing the heavy burdens and responsibilities that come with that crown. A **Destiny Quitter** is one who is unable to bear the weight of her crown, and rejects those burdens and responsibilities.

"She wears a crown built from her spine of inner strength and modesty. With sparkling jewels to represent each and every quality." **~ By Michelle Schaper**

When you are holding a position of power and privilege you may encounter any of the following conflicting voices and it is up to you to decide which voice will be loudest in defining you.

1. THE VOICE OF A WINNER OR THE VOICE OF A LOSER

You are DEFINED to choose between a voice that tells you to take responsibility that comes with power and privilege or a voice that tells you to abscond and abdicate from responsibility.

A **Destiny Queen** understands that having the privilege of a powerful position comes with heavy responsibilities.

A **Destiny Quitter** is one who wants to enjoy the privilege and power of her position but without the responsibilities that comes with it.

A **Destiny Queen** accepts and embraces her post and she positions herself there, ready to take up her responsibilities.

Whereas a **Destiny Quitter** is one who rejects her post and she depositions herself from there to escape her responsibilities.

There is a story in the bible (book of Esther) of two queens who both found themselves in strategic privileged positions. Each queen faced a serious crisis and dilemma. In the case of the first queen (Vashti), her king demanded that she parade herself dressed in a demeaning manner before a multitude during a royal banquet. In the case of the second queen (Esther), her King was being misled to follow the advice of this queen's enemies to discriminate against her people and annihilate them.

This second queen (Esther) immediately recognized her advantage and the power of her position and she decided to confront the crisis and to use her powerful position to avert the crisis despite the great risks involved. She defiantly said "If I die, I die; if I perish, I perish!"

However, the first queen (Vashti) underestimated the power of her privileged position and she assumes that she is helpless and cannot turn her crisis around and she doesn't even try and instead she bows out and throws in her crown.

"The most common way people give up their power is by thinking they don't have any." ~ **Alice Walker**

The problem with women who are like this first queen is that they fail to realize that no matter how negative a situation is and no matter how heavy the odds are against them in that situation, they always have an opportunity to see how they can turn it around for their good and for the good of the people relying on them, if only they could look hard enough for the appropriate strategies.

The first queen (Vashti) in our story could have responded to the demeaning and humiliating request of the king by not rejecting it but by using her privileged position to turn the heart of the king away from that which was meant to work against her. She could have sought a way to turn his heart towards that which would work in her favour, the way the second queen did.

It is unfortunate that this first queen (Vashti) appears to have belittled the powerful privileged position and she took it for granted. Either she had gotten it easily or she had already come from a powerful privileged background. This position was not such a big deal and therefore she could afford to lose it just as easy as she had got it.

We often do not value those things that have not cost us. The second queen (Esther) may have come from an underprivileged oppressed background without power and so she felt honoured to hold this position because she knew she got it by sheer grace. Her position came with a price and a Purpose and therefore she could not afford to take it for granted. She had a revelation that there was a significant reason why she had got this privileged position and she was supposed to fulfil some Purpose with this privileged position for a greater goal and legacy.

Which voices within and around you speak loudest when your privileged position of power demands your attention? Is it the voice of the first queen or the second?

Your ability to understand that privilege and power comes with responsibility is a key factor in enabling you to choose the right voices that will shape your identity and influence you through your journey to Destiny.

2. THE VOICE OF YOUR DESTINY HELPERS OR THE VOICE OF YOUR DESTINY DESTROYERS

You are DEFINED to choose between the voice of your Destiny helpers or the voice of your Destiny destroyers.

"The biggest help God can give you is the help of knowing who your Destiny helpers are and how to avoid losing them no matter what" ~ **Dr. Sony Badu**

A **Destiny Queen** understands that at her place of Purpose there are people and relationships who are her Destiny helpers to whom she must connect so that they can help her to fulfil her Purpose.

So, she quickly identifies her mentors, connectors, helpers, burden carriers, gatekeepers, intercessors etc. who push and provoke her towards fulfilling her Purpose.

She is also careful to identify her Destiny killers, those who seek to obstruct and hinder her from fulfilling her Purpose like Destiny chokers, Destiny destroyers, assassinators, defilers etc. and she must strategize how to outsmart and silence them.

A **Destiny Quitter** on the other hand does not bother to identify the crucial people and relationships around her. Instead, she surrounds herself with people who do not understand Destiny nor do they understand her Calling. Therefore, they cannot advise her or propel her towards it. Instead, they ignorantly or some knowingly mislead her away from fulfilling her Destiny by flattering her, licking her stilettos and hanging around her as time wasters and idlers.

Instead of challenging her, they sadly help her wallow in self-pity so she retreats and abandons her assignment and takes the easy way out.

"A flatterer is a secret enemy" ~ **A Hungarian Proverb**

It is often said that a flatterer is the shadow of a fool. So, if you allow yourself to be surrounded with flatterers then sadly you are the fool.

For every Destiny Woman, there are Destiny helpers specifically ordained to help you at your ordained place of Purpose.

In your journey to Destiny, your ability to identify and connect to the right relationships and networks will enable you to choose the right voices that will define you and influence you towards fulfilling your Destiny. The topic on relationships and how they impact on your Destiny has been exhaustively dealt with in Book 2 of this series which is titled *"Your Positioning and Connecting."*

"We don't meet people by accident. They are meant to cross our path for a reason." **Unknown**

3. THE VOICE OF A RADICAL GAME CHANGER OR THE VOICE OF A LAZY LETHARGIC

You are DEFINED to choose between the voice of a radical game changer or the voice of a lazy lethargic.

"Be a game-changer, the world is full of players" ~ **Unknown**

A **Destiny Queen** devices strategies that she may use to fulfil her Purpose which she executes with a lot of wisdom and skill to mobilize and activate her people and to outsmart and outmaneuver her enemies and to overcome all hindrances and obstructions, so that she becomes the master of the game.

"She remembered who she was and the game changed" ~ **Lalah Delia**

But a **Destiny Quitter** sits back lethargically paralyzed without any game plan because she has already decided that the task is too hard for her, even before she has tried.

A **Destiny Queen** is a game changer because every situation she steps into she takes authority, transforms lives and foundations and leaves it better than she found it thereby fulfilling her Destiny and leaving a legacy.

Whereas a **Destiny Quitter** retreats from her place of Purpose, absconds from her responsibilities and never fulfils her Destiny and any legacy she leaves is a negative one.

For example, as stated earlier there were two queens, whereby the second queen (Esther) was a trend setter and a game changer ready for radical action operating by a radical faith and a resilience. She became unstoppable and ended up literally setting a trend where others had feared or failed to venture. She changed the game in every situation she stepped into whereas the first queen (Vashti) refused to take up her responsibilities and chose to act lazily when she was expected to bring about change.

Are you a game changer or a game loser? Which voices within and around you, shout the loudest when in your privileged powerful position, the game starts?

4. THE VOICE OF SELF-SACRIFICE OR THE VOICE OF SELF-PRESERVATION

You are DEFINED to choose between the voice of self-sacrifice or the voice of self-preservation.

"A human being has many divine qualities. But there has never been another unparalleled divine quality like man's self-sacrifice or can there ever be" ~ **Sri Chinmoy**

A **Destiny Queen** sees the bigger picture by understanding that her call and Purpose is not about herself but about others so she is selfless and others-oriented as she uses her power, privilege and position to take responsibility for the benefit of others.

She is ready to face any risk, suffer any pain and self-sacrifice herself for the sake of others.

Whereas a **Destiny Quitter** is self-focused and only sees what is in front of her and only what concerns her so she is selfish and self-oriented and only uses her position, privilege, and power for her own benefit and self-preservation.

The second queen (Esther) was ready to pay a great price for the sake of others because she was selfless and 'others'-oriented.

Your ability to accept that fulfilling Destiny entails taking great risks, suffering, paying a price, and incurring losses for the sake of others enables/empowers you in fulfilling it. This could be within your family, business, profession, leadership, including your Place of Assignment or in other sectors in your society.

5. THE VOICE FROM THE COURAGE ZONE OR THE VOICE FROM THE COMFORT ZONE

You are DEFINED to choose between the voice from the courage zone or the voice from the comfort zone.

"You can choose courage or you can choose comfort, but you cannot choose both" ~ **Brene Brown**

A **Destiny Queen** operates from the courage zone where she operates fearlessly and courageously overcoming every obstacle and hindrance in her way, silencing every enemy of her Destiny.

She faces and confronts her fears courageously, and she knows that her assignments will require great courage, so she dwells in the courage zone.

"Courage is resistance to fear, mastery of fear, not absence of fear" ~ **Mark Twain**

Whereas a **Destiny Quitter** operates from a comfort zone where she retreats and hides herself avoiding any pain, discomfort, hardship and suffering whatsoever and therefore resisting any assignment that could stretch or push her and move her out of her comfort zone.

"Great things never come out of the comfort zone." ~ **Unknown**

In the story we also see that the second queen (Esther) was a pillar of great courage who chose to move out of her comfort zone and step into the unknown courage zone.

She was an influencer who impacted her generation, society and nation. In contrast, the first queen (Vashti) preferred to remain in her comfort zone and to operate in fear and doubt, preferring to be a spectator instead of a participant. Consequently, she completely failed to make any positive impact on her generation, society and nation and she faded into obscurity.

"You will never make history in your comfort zone." ~ **Unknown**

A **Destiny Quitter** dies in the comfort zone where she thought she was saving herself.

"A comfort zone is a beautiful place but nothing ever grows there." ~ **Unknown**

On the other hand, a **Destiny Queen** thrives in the courage zone where she was ready to perish.

Your ability to step out of your comfort zone into the courage zone is a key factor in your ability to fulfil your Destiny because you will never change your life until you step out or your comfort zone and change begins at the end of your comfort zone.

6. THE VOICE THAT VOTES TO FULFIL DESTINY OR THE VOICE THAT VOTES TO ABORT DESTINY

You are DEFINED to choose between the voice of fulfilling Destiny or the voice of aborting Destiny.

A **Destiny Queen** lives to celebrate and to leave a positive legacy whereas a **Destiny Quitter** leaves to regret her aborted Destiny and leaves a negative legacy.

An example is the **Destiny Queen** who after accomplishing her assignment was celebrated for having fulfilled her Purpose whereas the **Destiny Quitter** suffered in oblivion after aborting her Purpose.

There is probably nothing more painful or regretful than discovering that you have a Purpose and Destiny to fulfil, embarking on it and then not fulfilling it just because you were not prepared to take up your responsibility and pay the price that comes with the territory and to see your substitute enter the scene and excel fabulously.

Perhaps it might have been better if you had not discovered that you had a Purpose and a Destiny and you had remained in ignorant bliss.

Many women today in the market place spend years seeking and lobbying for positions of privilege and power without understanding the responsibility those positions and privileges come with.

Consequently, when they do get there, they simply use the privilege and power for their own self-aggrandizement and for their own selfish agendas and they miserably fail to have any positive impact or influence while in those positions.

In fact, some of those positions are so powerful and the privileges so grand that if you do not understand the Purpose why you are holding those positions and having those privileges then chances are that power and privilege will destroy you.

A **Destiny Queen** is one who is very alert and cautious when stepping into a position of power and privilege because she understands the responsibilities and risks and expectations upon her. So, she steps into them with understanding and awareness and sets herself to fulfil her mandate knowing that it was never about her, but about a greater goal.

7. THE VOICE OF A VICTOR OR THE VOICE OF A VICTIM

You are DEFINED to choose between the voice leading you to travail in prayer as a Victor or the voice leading you to wallow in self-pity as a Victim.

A **Destiny Queen** immerses herself at the place of prayer travailing for empowerment in order to fulfil her Destiny while a **Destiny Quitter** fails to apply herself and prefers to recant her woes and tribulations to her idlers as she hosts pity parties.

We see that the second queen (Esther) had an anointing for intercession, divine favour, kingdom strategy and kingdom exploits and hence the reason she was able to fulfil her Purpose.

However, the first queen (Vashti), instead of interceding and seeking strategy chose the way of escape because deep down she was lazy and did not want to apply herself and probably also because she knew that intercession was work and that it came at a cost which she was not ready to pay.

As a **Destiny Queen** you have been ordained to be a prayer warrior, an intercessor, a gatekeeper and a watchman and it will be very different for you to fulfil your Destiny unless you build and sustain an altar of prayer.

"Prayer is the place of refuge for every worry, a foundation for cheerfulness, a source of constant happiness, a protection against sadness." **~ St. John Chrysostom**

So, you must learn to dwell in your secret place of prayer from where you will receive empowerment, find clarity, direction, revelation and insight.

It is only at your place of prayer that you will receive the strategies that you need in order to fulfil your Purpose and Destiny.

It is a misconception for us to think that education and intellectualism on their own is sufficient, or to be misguided into believing that being connected to powerful people and networks is all that is needed to fulfil Destiny. The truth is that prayer is a fundamental tool and ingredient that everyone needs in order to fulfil her Destiny.

"Never doubt the power of prayer" **~Unknown**

Destiny Questions to Ponder On

1. *What is the significance of a crown in your opinion?*

2. *How would you distinguish between the voice of one helping you to fulfil your Destiny and one obstructing you from fulfilling your Destiny?*

3. *In which instances have you been a radical game changer and in which have you been a lazy lethargic?*

4. *How would you differentiate between self-sacrifice and self-preservation?*

5. *How do you get out of a comfort zone?*

6. *In which other ways are you likely to abort your Destiny?*

7. *Are you often a Victor or a Victim?*

This Page Was Intentionally Left Blank

Chapter Six

THE DESTINY PRESERVER OR DESTINY DESTROYER

Relocating and Realigning Yourself For Destiny

Chapter Preview

1. *A voice to thrive or a voice to perish.*

2. *A voice to seize opportunities or a voice to remain indifferent*

3. *A voice to make a radical shift or a voice to lag behind*

4. *A voice to master your Destiny or a voice to enslave your Destiny*

5. *A voice to leave a positive legacy or a voice to leave a negative legacy.*

6. *A voice that directs you to your Destiny or a voice that distracts you from your Destiny*

7. *A voice that protects and supports the Destiny of others or a voice that derails and sabotages the Destiny of others.*

OPENING REMARKS

In the course of your quest to fulfil your Destiny you may find yourself wrongly positioned whether physically, mentally, emotionally or spiritually etc. This means that due to either wrong choices and decisions or even factors beyond your control you end up in a wrong lifestyle, wrong career and occupation and wrong relationships etc. A place where the environment is not conducive for your well-being, so your real identity, potential and Destiny remain suffocated, stifled and locked up within you. Sometimes you may not even know it until something happens to make you realize that you are wrongly positioned in a place where you will never be able to discover or fulfil your Destiny.

Another scenario is where you encounter people of Destiny or regimes and systems that are Destiny oriented and you must make a radical choice whether to support and protect those carriers of Destiny and preserve their Destiny or to neglect or derail their Destiny.

Then you must arise and make a radical Destiny choice whether to remain there and derail your Destiny or make a swift move and preserve your Destiny.

Your choice either way will not only impact on your own Destiny but on the Destiny of many others who are tied and connected to you as well as on future generation in your lineage. To this extent you become either a **Destiny Preserver** or a **Destiny Destroyer**.

Sometimes a **Destiny Destroyer** means well but she is sincerely misguided for example in the case of a parent who thinks she is preserving or protecting the Destiny of her child by the choices she makes for that child (whether it is in terms of career, education, culture and relationships) but unknown to her she is derailing that child from its Destiny. So, the line between preserving and derailing can sometimes be very thin. So, you must watch your actions and audit what voices you listen to when it comes to the choices you make for your child or the choices you allow your child to make.

A **Destiny Preserver** therefore is one who decides to come out of the wrong place where she is at and to move to a right and better place in order to preserve her own Destiny and the Destiny of others. While a **Destiny Destroyer** is one who chooses to remain in the wrong place and fails to move to the right and better place and she thereby derails her own Destiny and the Destiny of others.

1. CHOOSING BETWEEN THE VOICE TO THRIVE OR THE VOICE TO PERISH

You are DEFINED to choose between the voice leading you to move to an environment, where your Destiny will thrive and be preserved or the voice leading you to remain in the wrong environment, where your Destiny will be derailed.

A **Destiny Preserver** will always be restless and dissatisfied when in a wrong place or environment that is not provoking her to become the very best of herself and to be the very best at what she does and thereby fulfil her Destiny.

Whereas a **Destiny Destroyer** is one who is oblivious of her wrong environment and is content to live in mediocrity, never aspiring for more so as she derails her own Destiny, she thwarts and undermines the Destiny of others in the process.

As a Destiny Woman you must constantly assess the place where you are at whether physically, emotionally, socially, occupationally, intellectually, spiritually, environmentally etc. so as to ascertain whether you are in an inferior place where your Destiny is stifled and derailed and if so, you must Purpose to relocate.

There is a story of two women in the bible **(Joshua 2 & Judges 16)** who were living an undesirable lifestyle. The first one was a potential **Destiny Preserver** living in a place of death without Purpose and Destiny. When she encountered people of Destiny, she immediately discerned and identified with them and the Destinies they were carrying.

She was ready to go to great lengths and take great risks to preserve them and their destinies from being destroyed. By virtue of doing so, she was able to mentally and emotionally and later physically relocate to the right place where she knew she would have a Destiny. She chose to uproot herself and leave her current place of death where she had no Destiny. Her name was Rahab the harlot.

The second Woman was a potential **Destiny Destroyer**. When she encountered a man of Destiny, she went out of her way at the behest of her wicked people to derail the man of Destiny. By virtue of derailing the man and his Destiny, she herself never got a chance to relocate from the place of death and never fulfilled any Destiny. Her name was Delilah.

Beware that you are not like the second Woman when you encounter people of Destiny. Beware you are not influenced by Destiny haters around you to derail Destiny people that you encounter. Instead allow those Destiny people to impact you like the first Woman. In preserving and protecting them, you will yourself locate to a better place and fulfil your Destiny.

2. CHOOSING BETWEEN THE VOICE TO SEIZE OPPORTUNITIES OR THE VOICE TO REMAIN INDIFFERENT

You are DEFINED to choose between a voice leading you to seize opportunities versus a voice leading you to be indifferent and disinterested.

A **Destiny Preserver** recognizes her hour of visitation. She is proactive in taking quick and timely action in laying hold of opportunities that present themselves to her and her entry into Destiny doors.

"Success in life hinges more on seizing opportunity than having everything go as planned." ~ **Ethan Austin**

Whereas a **Destiny Destroyer** is numb to her hour of visitation and is blinded to any opportunities around her and remains in a state of inactivity, unable to make any positive progress.

"Opportunities are like sunrises. If you wait too long, you miss them." ~ **William Arthur Ward**

For example, the first Woman, Rahab, (the **Destiny Preserver**), knew she had to act quickly because the window of opportunity would not remain open forever. So, in wisdom she quickly made a covenant with her benefactors in order to secure her interests and the interests of her family.

The second Woman Delilah, had several windows of opportunity to side with the man of Destiny (Samson) and align with that which would be more beneficial to her but she misused the opportunity.

As a Woman of Destiny, you must be constantly alert to discern opportunities no matter how they are packaged and to seize those opportunities so that they may empower you into fulfilling your Destiny. Anyone who adopts a laid-back attitude in their journey to Destiny will always miss the train.

3. CHOOSING BETWEEN THE VOICE TO MAKE A RADICAL SHIFT OR THE VOICE TO LAG BEHIND

You are DEFINED to choose between the voice leading you to make a radical shift and relocation and the voice leading you to remain stagnant in one place.

A **Destiny Preserver** is one who recognizes the right timing for making a change in her location in order to move to a better location where there is a better and more conducive environment to fulfil her Purpose and enter her Destiny.

A **Destiny Preserver** recognizes when the time comes to disconnect from a place that is not conducive to her welfare and that is not empowering her to fulfil her Purpose and that keeps her disadvantaged, shunned and discriminated against.

The second Woman, Delilah (the **Destiny Destroyer**), when approached by a man of influence, she just continued to be dishonest and ended up destroying the man. Thus, she prejudiced herself and a whole generation, because she failed to take the opportunity to help that man who would have to radically changed her life for the better. In contrast, the first Woman, Rahab, went through a paradigm shift by virtue of the choice and decision she made in her hour of visitation. In the process she preserved the Destiny of the spies who were Destiny carriers and preserved the Destiny of a whole generation.

Your journey to Destiny will entail constant radical shifts and relocations. You must always be able to discern when such a radical shift is required. More importantly, you must be prepared to make it because your Destiny and location are related.

4. CHOOSING BETWEEN THE VOICE TO MASTER YOUR DESTINY OR A VOICE TO ENSLAVE

You are DEFINED to choose between a voice leading you to take charge and be the master of your Destiny or the voice leading you to allow others to dictate and control your Destiny.

A **Destiny Preserver** is one who becomes the master of her Destiny and sets the course of her life, changes the direction where need be.

A **Destiny Preserver** exercises her power of choice by weighing the risks and the opportunities and then making the right choices that will feed her Purpose and enable her to fulfil her Purpose because she bases her choices on the right considerations.

A **Destiny Preserver** knows when to correct her wrong choices and to redirect her life in the right direction in order to preserve her Destiny.

Whereas a **Destiny Destroyer** remains a pawn in the hands of others.

Let us revisit the example of the two women (the **Destiny Preserver** and the **Destiny Destroyer**). While the first Woman, Rahab was ready to escape the kind of background that kept her yoked and enslaved to the desires of men, the second Woman Delilah was not so ready to break the enslavement.

Consequently, the first Woman Rahab was able to take charge of her Destiny by fulfilling a very important Purpose that positively impacted future generations. While the second Woman Delilah retreated into oblivion as a Woman who destroyed the Destiny of another and negatively impacted the future generations.

You must constantly remember that you are the captain and master of your Destiny. Unless you take charge of it, you will not fulfil it. The passion for your Destiny cannot be imposed on you nor can anyone take the risks and handle the responsibilities that come with your Destiny on your behalf.

Most importantly, no one can make the Destiny decisions and choices which are crucial in the fulfilment of your Destiny on your behalf.

5. CHOOSING BETWEEN A VOICE TO LEAVE A POSITIVE LEGACY OR A VOICE TO LEAVE A NEGATIVE LEGACY

You are DEFINED to choose between a voice leading you to be intentional and leave a positive legacy or the voice leading you to be indifferent and leave a negative legacy.

A **Destiny Preserver** is deliberate and intentional in the fulfilment of the Purpose ensuring that she runs her own race in her own lane and that she not only finishes her race but she finishes strong and leaves a positive legacy that impacts generations and lineages.

"All good men and women must take responsibility to create legacies that will take the next generation to a level we could only imagine."
~Jim Rohn

Whereas a **Destiny Destroyer** lacks the commitment and focus to discover and fulfil her own Purpose. So, she does not only derail herself but she ends up derailing others and thereby leaves a negative legacy that threatens the welfare of generations and lineages.

Both the women in our story were history makers even though we remember one positively and the other negatively. The first Woman chose to leave a positive legacy behind while the second just went on and ended up leaving a negative legacy.

Destiny is about leaving a legacy and if you have followed the laid down principles and adhered to all that is required, chances are you will leave a very positive legacy. Destiny is always about having a positive impact and benefit for people, societies, nations and yourself.

So, when you have gone out of your way to preserve people and their destinies then you will leave a good legacy. Where you have been negligent and malicious in derailing people's destinies then you will leave a negative legacy.

6. CHOOSING BETWEEN THE VOICE OF YOUR DESTINY HELPERS OR THE VOICE OF YOUR DESTINY KILLERS

You are DEFINED to choose between a voice leading you to align and connect yourself with your Destiny Relationships and Helpers or a voice leading you to align yourself with toxic Relationships and Killers.

A **Destiny Preserver** goes out of her way to seek and identify the people of her Purpose and then connects to those relationships. She recognizes their value and their role in helping her fulfil her Destiny so she guards them, maintains them and nurtures them.

She understands the power of covenant and that they come with benefits and responsibilities and that her covenant relationships will connect and transition her into better and valuable things.

"Keeping covenants protects us, prepares us, and empowers us." ~ **Rosemary M. Wixom**

A **Destiny Preserver** understands which people are relevant in a particular season and dispensation and who are headed in the right direction. So that she aligns with such people and disconnects with the wrong people who are headed in the wrong direction and are not relevant in that dispensation and season.

The **Destiny Destroyer** remains in dysfunctional and toxic relationships that misuse and mislead her into messing her own Destiny and more tragically into derailing the Destiny of others.

The first Woman, Rahab (the **Destiny Preserver**), distinguishes herself from a, Delilah (the **Destiny Destroyer**). A day comes when the **Destiny Preserver** is approached by people of influence who were carriers of Destiny and her choice to align herself with them radically changes her life forever and shifts her from her previous toxic and destructive relationships to relationships that had power to usher her to Destiny.

However, with the second Woman Delilah when a day came and she was approached by a man of influence who was a carrier of Destiny. Her choice to be dishonest with him instead of aligning herself with the greatness within him caused her to remain among her toxic relationships that had no power to usher her to Destiny.

Relationships are the engine to Destiny and they are a fundamental tool in enabling you to fulfil your Destiny. You must be able to discern and identify your Destiny covenant relationships no matter how they are packaged, to develop those relationships and to maintain them, understanding clearly how each relationship impacts on your Destiny.

7. CHOOSING BETWEEN THE VOICE TO PROTECT AND SUPPORT THE DESTINY OF OTHERS OR THE VOICE TO DERAIL AND SABOTAGE THE DESTINY OF OTHERS

You are DEFINED to choose between a voice leading you to support, protect and preserve people, regimes and systems that carry Destiny or a voice leading you to derail, sabotage and destroy such people, regimes and systems.

A **Destiny Preserver** recognizes people, regimes and systems that are carrying Destiny and that are headed in the right direction and building the right foundations. Rahab discerned that the spies were Destiny carriers sent by a Destiny regime and hence her choice to protect and preserve them.

A **Destiny Preserver** is always ready to defeat the enemies of Destiny (irrespective of how closely she may have been related to them previously) because she realizes she had been connected to the wrong people who had no capacity to usher her and propel her to her Destiny. Sometimes you must shift alliances and allegiances for the sake of your Destiny.

The first Woman, Rahab is a protector and a guardian of the people of Destiny and that which matters. The second Woman Delilah is a destroyer of the people of Destiny and that which matters.

In your journey to Destiny, you will encounter various types of regimes, cultures and systems, and you must be able to identify those ones that promote the Destiny of people as opposed to those that oppose and oppress the Destiny of people and listen to the voice telling you to protect and preserve them.

Destiny Questions to Ponder On

1. *How do you distinguish between an environment where you are thriving and an environment where you are perishing?*
2. *What obstructs you from seizing opportunities in a given situation?*
3. *What are the dangers of remaining stagnant in one place?*
4. *How do you become the master of your Destiny?*
5. *How do you leave a positive legacy?*
6. *How do you identify your Destiny helpers?*
7. *How do you identify the people and the regimes whose destinies you need to preserve?*

This Page Was Intentionally Left Blank

Chapter Seven

THE DESTINY CLINGER OR DESTINY KISSER

Making The Right Choices At Critical

Crossroads

Chapter Preview

1. *The voice leading you to a place of fruitfulness or the voice leading you to remain in a place of barrenness.*

2. *The voice of death or the voice of life.*

3. *The voice of change or the voice of stagnation.*

4. *The voice of divine connection or the voice of carnal connections.*

5. *The voice of a new season or the voice of an outdated season.*

6. *The voice of proactivity or the voice of passivity.*

7. *The experienced voice of wise counsel or the inexperienced voice of misguided counsel.*

OPENING REMARKS

At one time or another in the course of fulfilling your Destiny you will be faced with various dilemmas in various situations and circumstances and how you resolve those dilemmas will be determined by the voices within and around you that you have permitted to define and influence you.

A **Destiny Clinger** is one who listens to the right voices and therefore clings to her Destiny.

Pro.19:20 – *"Listen to counsel and receive instruction, that you may be wise in your latter days."*

While a **Destiny Kisser** is one who listens to the wrong voices and therefore aborts her Destiny, by turning her back to it and by kissing it goodbye.

In your journey to Destiny, you will inevitably suffer some losses like the loss of very valuable and meaningful relationships and associations. Whether through physical or emotional separation or actual death, whether it be within the family, your social networks, your divine spiritual connections, your business and professional colleagues etc. You are left devastated. This is because the value they added and the significance and relevance they held in your life in terms of your emotional, spiritual or financial support etc. In your mind you thought that those relationships were the ones from which you would conceive and birth your success or even Destiny so you go into a confusion and desperation wondering which way forward.

Sometimes it could be that the loss and death of those relationships happened in a place or environment that now represents loss, pain and death for you. In addition, it could also be a place where you experienced dryness and barrenness as you did not bear any fruit and you have nothing to show for all the time spent there, so that place also represents barrenness for you whether it was a place of your business enterprise, career, church ministry or family set up. You therefore reach a "Destiny crossroad" when you must decide whether to remain there or move on.

Perhaps what you should note so as to enable you make a decision once you reach this Destiny crossroad, is that maybe you had positioned yourself in the wrong place and in the wrong relationships hence the loss, pain and death.

1. CHOOSING BETWEEN THE VOICE LEADING YOU TO A PLACE OF FRUITFULNESS OR THE VOICE HOLDING YOU AT A PLACE OF BARRENNESS

You are DEFINED by choosing between a voice leading you to flee to a place of life and fruitfulness and a voice leading you to remain in that place of loss and death.

A **Destiny Clinger** is one who has encountered loss and tragedy and carries with her a stigma, but she understands what and who she needs to cling to in order to break her barrenness and relocate to her fruitfulness.

She is one who is able to make quick decisions when she is at a crossroad. She purposefully wipes her tears from her pain of loss and tragedy (lest they blind her to seeing properly what is around her) and she makes a quick and right decision.

"Life presents you with so many decisions. A lot of times, they're right in front of your face and they're really difficult, but we must make them." ~ **Brittany Murphy**

She is one who has already decided that the place where she is at, where she has suffered so much loss and tragedy cannot possibly be the right place for her. So after quickly climbing out of the dark pit of tragedy, loss and trauma, she makes a quick mental calculation of the options ahead of her and she quickly decides to take charge of the direction in which her life will take.

Whereas a **Destiny Kisser** is one who has similarly undergone tragedy and loss and also carries with her the stigma. She does not understand who or what she needs to cling to, in order to break her barrenness and relocate to her fruitfulness.

Instead, she allows her tears and sorrow to blind her from clearly seeing her situation and she fails to climb out of the dark pit quickly enough in order to calculate her next move. In the process she sadly fails to make the right decisions and choices and remains in her place of barrenness.

A story is written in the bible (in the Book of Ruth) of two women both at a crossroad. They needed to make decisions that would make or break their Destiny. They were to either remain located at their place of loss and death or to depart from it.

The first Woman, was called Ruth, (the **Destiny Clinger**), who had the hope and faith that somehow her situation would change for the better even though she didn't have any idea how.

So, she chose to depart from her place of loss, barrenness and death and relocate to a place of life and fruitfulness, by clinging to her mother-in-law Naomi. Even though her husband Naomi's son had died in that place of death leaving her barren nonetheless, deep within her she discerned that relocating to a place of life and fruitfulness might miraculously lead her to another husband. This is one of the greatest stories about Destiny that everyone should read The Other Woman called Orpah, (the **Destiny Kisser**), had no flicker of hope or faith and was completely blinded to any possibility of her situation changing for the better.

In our journey to Destiny some of our relationships will die. We must learn to differentiate between those relationships that cannot be resurrected so that we can move on swiftly to identify and connect to new relationships so that we can accomplish the Purposes we were created for.

2. CHOOSING BETWEEN THE VOICE OF DEATH OR THE VOICE OF LIFE

You are DEFINED by choosing between a voice leading you to wash off the foul stench of death OR a voice leading you to immerse yourself in that foul stench of death.

A **Destiny Clinger** is one who has faced the tragedy of death of loved ones or of things she held dear (like a business empire, a church ministry, a prospective career or lucrative positions of leadership and power). She finds herself grieving with despair and hopelessness because of the significance of those people and things in her life.

"The irony of grief is that the identity you need to talk to about how you feel is the identity who is no longer here." ~ **Unknown**

However, she quickly realizes that in order for her to get out of her hopelessness, she must wash off the foul stench of death and take off the weight and heaviness of her mourning garments so she can see clearly and move on without any baggage.

"The reality is that you will grieve forever. You will not 'get over' the loss of a loved one; you will learn to live with it. You will heal and you will rebuild yourself around the loss." ~ **Elisabeth Kubler**

She then gets a flicker of hope that perhaps it is not the end of the world. She may not know how the people and things she has lost can be replaced. Yet deep in her she believes and knows that relocating from the place where she lost them (both emotionally and physically) is the answer to her locating the place where she will get their replacements and recompense.

Whereas a **Destiny Kisser** is one who has similarly faced the tragedy of death of loved ones and things. She finds herself grieving with despair and hopelessness because of the significance of those people and things. So, she despairs but instead of washing off the foul stench of death she chooses to immerse herself in it and remains in her grief. She becomes too wounded to entertain any hope that she could ever find other people and things. So, she remains buried and suffocated in her mourning garments and she fails to see any hope or light at the end of the tunnel.

The **Destiny Clinger** therefore relocates to her place of life and fruitfulness without any foul stench of death upon her enabling her to make a fresh start and to ultimately fulfil her Destiny. The **Destiny Kisser** however remains at her place of death, loss and barrenness and never fulfils any Destiny.

3. CHOOSING BETWEEN THE VOICE OF CHANGE OR THE VOICE OF STAGNATION

You are DEFINED by choosing between a voice leading you to transition or a voice leading you to remain in stagnation.

A **Destiny Clinger** is one who quickly understands that she is at a crossroad and that a time for inevitable change has come whether or not she is ready. She recognizes that she must undergo a process of transitioning (both physically and emotionally) from the place of barrenness, death, despair and hopelessness.

She knows that she needs to locate another place where hopefully her barrenness will be broken, the dead things in her life will be replaced and she will be able to fulfil her Purpose and enter Destiny. Although she may not know or have any guarantees about the new place, she seeks to locate to she nonetheless steps forward by faith because she cannot remain where she is.

She understands that this time of transition is a time of changes and crisis that she must learn how to manage. That it is a place of opportunities and options. More importantly, that it is a Destiny defining moment where whatever choice she makes will be the difference between fulfilling or aborting her Purpose.

She knows she's at a place called "Crossroad Choices" otherwise known as "Destiny dilemmas". She chooses to cling to the little she knows about where she is going and to those who know about the place where she is going. She realizes those people will be instrumental in her redemption at that new place.

"When shifts and transitions in life shake you to the core, see that as a sign of the greatness that's about to occur." ~ **Chelsea Dinen**

Whereas a **Destiny Kisser** chooses to remain smothered in the foul stench of death and her eyes remained blurred by the tears of her barrenness. She fails to embrace the opportunity for transition, she harbours negative mind-set towards change even without first analyzing the facts. So, she ends up stepping back and retreating into the place of death and barrenness (physically and emotionally). In the process of doing so, she has made a Destiny choice whereby she ends up missing any chance for fulfilling Purpose and she becomes relegated to oblivion.

"Stagnation is death. If you don't change, you die. It's that simple. It's that scary." ~ **Leonard Sweet**

The **Destiny Clinger** having seen the flicker of hope out of her desperate situation made a Destiny decision to relocate from the place of death and barrenness to a place of life and abundance even though at this point she has no guarantees (which makes her decision a radical one out of a radical faith).

The **Destiny Clinger** is one who makes wise choices in a time of crisis leading her to lay hold of opportunities that usher her into her miracles and blessings (whether it be in business, career, leadership, church ministry or family life).

However, the **Destiny Kisser** is one who makes the wrong choices by failing to transition and thereby misses any opportunities that were in front of her and ultimately failing to fulfil Purpose and enter Destiny.

Your inability to manage your transitions effectively and wisely will often lead to an abortion of Purpose.

4. CHOOSING BETWEEN THE VOICE OF DIVINE CONNECTIONS OR THE VOICE OF CARNAL CONNECTIONS

You are DEFINED by choosing between a voice leading you to connect to your Destiny helpers who carry greatness OR a voice leading you to disconnect from such people.

A **Destiny Clinger** is one who recognizes that among the people she has been surrounding herself with, there are those who carry greatness and potential. She identifies with that greatness and potential somehow knowing that they have what it takes to usher her to a new place where her barrenness will be broken and her dead things will be replaced.

So, she chooses to see beyond where those people are at in that moment and she chooses to see where they are headed. She chooses not to see their current character flaws where they are full of dysfunctions and weaknesses and instead, she chooses to see the potential and greatness within them that is being covered up by their current dysfunctions and weaknesses.

A **Destiny Clinger** recognizes the right Destiny relationships necessary for her Purpose and Destiny because at this point, she has washed off the stench of death and the tears from the pain of her barrenness and loss.

She is able to see with clarity the relationships around her. She is able to see them from a deep perspective as opposed to seeing them from a shallow superficial perspective.

In addition, a **Destiny Clinger** is one who is loyal to people who have been good to her and who have helped her and she is often very reluctant to abandon them in their hour of need (even when they may not seem to need her).

A clinger also understands that more often than not she may be the one who needs those people and not the other way around or at any rate they both need each other.

Whereas a **Destiny Kisser** fails to discern which are the covenant Destiny relationships around her. She chooses to see them superficially and judges them by their dysfunctions and small beginnings believing that they do not have the capacity to make a way for her out of her hopelessness and despair.

In this story the **Destiny Clinger** (Ruth), immediately discerned who Naomi (her mother-in-law) was and the potential in her to usher her to a better place. So, she seized the opportunity and chose to cling to her and follow her. The **Destiny Clinger** did not allow her mother-in-law's bitterness or her apparent hopelessness to blind her to the potential within Naomi to usher her to a better place.

A **Destiny Clinger** understands second chances and new beginnings. She discerns that for every clinger there has to be a Destiny helper or a Destiny connector (namely someone ordained to walk her through her second chance and usher her to her new beginning and ultimately to her Destiny).

Destiny Clinger identifies and connects to her Destiny helpers and Destiny connectors. She is one who is ready to submit to legitimate, authentic authority in her life, and to obey instructions and heed wise counsel that will break her barrenness and propel her to Destiny.

However, the **Destiny Kisser** Orpah failed to discern who Naomi (her mother-in-law) was, and did not see the potential in her to help her. She allowed her mother-in-law's bitterness and hopelessness to blind her so she therefore chose to kiss her goodbye.

A **Destiny Kisser** is one whose Destiny helper and connector is right in front of her but is unable to discern that. She is too blinded by sorrow and past pain. So, she despises and fails to connect to her Destiny helpers and Destiny connectors thereby missing her second chance and new beginning and ultimately her Destiny.

5. CHOOSING BETWEEN THE VOICE OF A NEW SEASON OR A VOICE OF AN OUTDATED SEASON.

You are DEFINED by choosing between a voice leading you to step out in to a new season OR a voice leading you to remain in the outdated season.

A **Destiny Clinger** knows that after she makes her Destiny choices at her crossroads during her defining moment. She must then take action because decisions alone are not sufficient and failure to take action may cause her to retreat or remain stagnant.

A **Destiny Clinger** decides in her mind, then she speaks it in her mouth declaring and confessing it because she knows the power of her words that will seal her decision. Then she takes action thereby effectively managing the change and process of transition.

Whereas a **Destiny Kisser** either makes the wrong decision in her mind then she speaks that wrong decision in her mouth. She ends up taking the wrong action. Alternatively in her paralysis, she fails to make any decision in her mind. She fails to speak anything to show what she has decided and, in the process, her failure to decide and speak ends up being a decision and choice in itself (namely a choice not to make a choice).

A **Destiny Kisser** fails to step out into the new beginning out of fear, wrong choice or lack of choice at all and remains in the very place where she encountered barrenness, death and loss. In the process she kisses her Destiny goodbye.

"Do something uncomfortable today. By stepping out of your box, you don't have to settle for what you are — you get to create who you want to become." **~ Howard Walstein**

A **Destiny Kisser** is one who is easily dissuaded from making the right decisions because she is looking for what she feels is the easier way out, whether consciously or subconsciously.

Ruth, the **Destiny Clinger** chose to step out by faith not knowing what lay ahead of her but knowing that whatever it was, it had to be better than what she was stepping out of. In the end her radical decision paid off.

Whereas Orpah the **Destiny Kisser**, was too fearful or lethargic to take a step of faith and she chose to remain in the old (even though deep down) she must have known that there was no hope in a place where she had already encountered such pain, loss and death.

6. CHOOSING BETWEEN THE VOICE OF PROACTIVITY OR THE VOICE OF PASSIVITY.

You are DEFINED by choosing between a voice leading you to be proactive OR a voice leading you to be passive.

A **Destiny Clinger** understands that the journey to fulfilling Purpose and entering Destiny is a process and not an overnight event. She understands that she must accept and embrace that process because it prepares and equips her for that Purpose and Destiny.

She understands the need for wise counsel from midwives, mentors, Destiny helpers and connectors who she understands have more experience than she has because they have travelled a path she has not. So, she knows she needs them and she must trust and rely on them.

Once a **Destiny Clinger** locates her place of Purpose, she positions herself proactively by seeing what needs to be done in order to establish herself in that place. She knows she must take responsibility in safeguarding her Destiny and the Destiny of her people, taking charge and responsibility as she waits for things to unfold.

"Being active every day makes it easier to hear that inner voice." ~ **Haruki Murakami**

However, a **Destiny Kisser** prefers to be passive and will often throw in the towel because positioning and establishing herself in the place of Purpose may prove too difficult. She is not ready to apply herself and, in the process, she fails to fulfil her Purpose because she adopts a self-pity attitude.

"Progress rarely comes as a result of being passive." ~ **Marc Morial**

Ruth (the **Destiny Clinger**) in our story as she stepped into her new beginning, she knew that there would be a process to go through before she could lay hold of her miracle and blessings.

She therefore humbly submitted herself to that process and found herself in the gleaning field, busy applying herself and using whatever skills and resources within her to survive. She looked around and stepped into the opportunities that were available to her as opposed to sitting back in self-pity.

Often in our journey to Destiny, and after we have managed to escape from the old into the new, we may deceive ourselves into thinking that our blessing will happen automatically overnight. We fail to realize that we must undergo the process of the new place (whether that place comes with new relationships, a new career, a new position, a new business etc.). So, in the process we are moulded and we acquire the capacity to handle and thrive in that new place and in that new thing.

We must be ready to allow the seasons in that new beginning to mould and sculpture us until we are finally ready to lay hold of our blessings in that new place.

7. CHOOSING BETWEEN THE EXPERIENCED VOICE OF WISE COUNSEL OR THE INEXPERIENCED VOICE OF MISGUIDED COUNSEL

You are DEFINED by choosing between a voice leading you to submit and embrace the instructions of your Destiny midwives and helpers OR a voice leading you to take matters into your own hands.

A **Destiny Clinger** is one who finds herself in a situation she has not faced before. She starts relying totally on the advice and instructions of her mentors, midwives and Destiny helpers so as to know what she needs to lay hold of. Even though in her heart she is a little apprehensive as to whether taking their bold and radical instructions will work or backfire.

She recognizes that those advising her have been there before so they must know what they are talking about. Yet she is still apprehensive because some of the instructions from her helpers may require her to take action that she fears may cause her shame and ridicule. Yet she soon overcomes her self-consciousness and any fear of shame and humiliation. She realizes that she must be ready to take whatever risks she must on her reputation in order to move forward.

A **Destiny Clinger** is always too passionate about Destiny to care about people's opinions or about her reputation. She knows fulfilling her Purpose and Destiny comes with a price and sacrifice. So, she operates in radical obedience and radical faith.

Whereas a **Destiny Kisser** will be too self-conscious to take any step she's not sure of or to take any action that she fears may embarrass shame or humiliate her. She is not ready to be uncomfortable in any situation and she is not ready to pay any price or make any sacrifices because she is not passionate enough for her Destiny.

When Ruth (the **Destiny Clinger)** was instructed by Naomi (her mother-in-law) to position herself in the threshing floor, she humbly submitted herself to that wise counsel. She knew this was a place she had not been before and a culture she had not experienced before. She therefore needed to trust her Naomi in order to get all the help, support and guidance that she needed.

Whenever you step into a new season and place, (with new positions, relationships or opportunities) you must allow your Destiny helpers to guide you in becoming established there because that new season and place comes with its challenges for which you need to be equipped by those with the relevant wisdom, experience, skills and expertise.

Destiny Questions to Ponder On

1. *How do you distinguish between a place of fruitfulness and a place of barrenness?*

2. *How do you distinguish between a place of life and a place of death?*

3. *How do you recognize the time for change and transition?*

4. *What other understanding do you have of divine connections?*

5. *How do you step out of an old season and into a new season?*

6. *What factors cause you to be passive when you should be proactive?*

7. *How do you locate those with wise counsel?*

This Page Was Intentionally Left Blank

Chapter Eight

THE DESTINY CONNECTOR OR THE DESTINY BLOCKER

Ushering Others To Their Destiny As You Enter Your Own

Chapter Preview

1. *A voice of knowledge or a voice of ignorance.*

2. *A voice of faith or a voice of fear and doubt*

3. *A voice that guards' relationships or a voice that destroys relationships.*

4. *A voice of wisdom and guidance as a mentor or a voice of one who misleads out of neglect.*

5. *A voice that heals past pain or a voice that holds on to past pain.*

6. *A voice that sheds light and truth or a voice that withholds the light and the truth.*

7. *A voice that ushers others to Destiny or a voice that focuses only on self.*

OPENING REMARKS

As a Woman of Destiny, you will definitely be equipped with various tools to fulfil that Destiny but your ability to use those tools effectively will be determined by the voices within and around you that you will listen to.

A **Destiny Connector** is one who invests in ushering others into their Destiny selflessly and in the process, she enters her own Destiny. A **Destiny Connector** is an intermediary between people and their Purpose and Destiny.

"The point about Connectors is that by having a foot in so many different worlds, they have the effect of bringing them all together." ~ **Malcolm Gladwell**

Just as you will have **Destiny Connector**s among your helpers, you will also be a **Destiny Connector** for many others. Your duty will be to announce of their gifts, talents, skills and potential to the right people and at strategic places at the appropriate time so as to usher them to their next level and ultimately to their Destiny.

On the other hand, a **Destiny Blocker** is one who either knowingly or unknowingly blocks her own Destiny and the Destiny of others by failing to play her role or by playing a contrary role.

"Watch out for blessing blockers: fear, anger, doubt, worry, regret, jealousy, and negative people." ~ **Karen Salmansohn**

Beware that you are not a **Destiny Blocker** whether knowingly or unknowingly to those people assigned to you.

A **Destiny Connector** is a life link to someone's future because they open doors and connect people to places and to other people that they need for their next level towards Destiny.

1. CHOOSING BETWEEN A VOICE OF KNOWLEDGE OR A VOICE OF IGNORANCE

You are DEFINED by choosing between a voice leading you to use crucial information and knowledge in your possession to connect someone to their Destiny OR to withhold that crucial information and knowledge and thereby block someone from their Destiny.

As a **Destiny Connector** you will often possess certain crucial information and knowledge or even be aware of a prophetic promise concerning the Destiny of someone who you have been assigned to usher to Destiny. This information and knowledge etc. is so crucial and necessary in guiding that person in their journey to Destiny.

So, when that person encounters a crisis and they become fearful (when their Destiny is under threat and attack in whatever circumstances) and you see that person about to make a wrong and hasty choice and decision that could be destructive to their Destiny then it is imperative upon you to disclose that knowledge and information etc. to that person. This is especially where that information and knowledge will protect them from making any wrong and hasty destructive decisions that could cost them their Destiny (or at any rate prejudice and jeopardize it by delaying it or putting it at risk). Your failure to do so is to become a **Destiny Blocker**.

The Purpose of disclosing that knowledge and information is a way of removing fear, confusion and despair. More importantly it as a way of building faith, hope and assurance so that the person can make the right choices and decisions based on the right information and knowledge.

A **Destiny Blocker** is one who either knowingly fails to disclose that crucial knowledge and information or if she does disclose it, she does so when it is too late and damage has already been caused. She is one who knowingly misinterprets that knowledge and information so that it causes more damage than harm to the Destiny of her protégé.

2. CHOOSING BETWEEN A VOICE OF FAITH OR A VOICE OF FEAR AND DOUBT

You are DEFINED by choosing between a voice leading you to feed Destiny people with faith and hope OR a voice leading you to feed Destiny people with fear and doubt.

"Hope is being able to see that there is light despite all of the darkness."
~ **Desmond Tutu**

A **Destiny Connector** is one who feeds her protégés with hope and faith about the future, and assures them that there is a place beyond their place of hopelessness where all is not lost.

A **Destiny Connector** is one who gives sound, solid credible and wise counsel calmly and constructively. She gives specific instructions and directions to enable her protégés to execute and implement those instructions towards locking into their Purpose and Destiny.

"You just need to have the guidance to lead you in the direction until you can do it yourself." ~**Tina Yothers**

A **Destiny Connector** expresses confidence that whatever counsel she is giving her protégé will bear fruit and bring the expected outcome. A **Destiny Connector**'s game plan is always based on truth and honesty thereby laying a proper foundation for her protégé's Destiny.

Whereas a **Destiny Blocker** is one who feeds her protégé with fear, panic and doubt because of her failure to disclose the facts and equip her protégés with sufficient understanding. Her advice is never well thought out but it is hectic and erratic thereby causing unnecessary anxiety.

A **Destiny Blocker** is never confident of herself or of what she is impacting on her protégé and any plan she devices is done so in deception and duplicity thereby laying a wrong foundation.

While the **Destiny Connector** (even in the midst of her own struggles, doubt and fear) is able to invest in the Destiny of another and usher them to their Destiny by being able to see the bigger picture and goal and somehow suspend her own struggles, doubts and fears.

3. CHOOSING BETWEEN A VOICE THAT GUARDS RELATIONSHIPS OR A VOICE THAT DESTROYS RELATIONSHIPS

You are DEFINED by choosing between a voice leading you to guard the relationships of your protégés OR a voice leading you to cause division and strife in those relationships.

A **Destiny Connector** knows that her most fundamental role is to connect her protégés to valuable relationships and to that extent she therefore ensures that she speaks well of her protégés. She speaks of their gifting and talents so as to guarantee them favour with those relationships she is connecting them to.

Her other role is to heal and mend any broken relationships and to restore connections where there has been broken connections between her protégés and those.

Destiny relationships (so as to ensure that the Destiny of her protégés are not prejudiced).

Whereas a **Destiny Blocker** causes strife and division between her protégés and valuable relationships either knowingly or unknowingly or by just being indifferent and insensitive and by failing to play her proper role of a connector.

In addition, a **Destiny Blocker** will often not be alert or sensitive to discern where there is strive and division. She will often not be concerned about restoring and reconciling her protégés with these important Destiny relationships.

A **Destiny Blocker** also plays favouritism and she becomes biased by preferring some of her protégés. In the process she causes jealousy among them which leads to strife and division, and thereby she becomes a blocker to all of them.

There is yet another story in the bible of two women who were both equipped to usher people to their destinies one was called Naomi (Book of Ruth) and the other was called Rebecca (Genesis 27). Naomi successfully ushered her protégé Ruth to Destiny by the honest and open methods she adopted, but Rebecca almost blocked the Destiny of her protégé by the dishonest methods and deceptive she adopted.

The **Destiny Connector** Naomi, was very wise in the way she approached her relative about the subject of a kinsman redeemer. She was very careful to ensure whether there had been any breach in the relationships among her relatives that could have jeopardized the kinsman redeemer concept. She appears to have been ready to bring a reconciliation or healing to the relationships if the need arose.

In other words, she understood the need to mend and maintain relationships for Purposes of her protégé's Destiny.

Whereas Rebecca the **Destiny Blocker** ended up causing friction between her two sons by favouring one. She used deceptive means to secure the interests of the one she favoured instead of allowing God to fulfil the promise he had already given concerning the chosen son in God's own way and in God's own time.

The friction she caused led to anger and bitterness and a long separation between the two brothers that almost aborted their destinies until God healed the relationship.

In your journey to Destiny, you must be careful to check whether those who are supposed to be connecting you (to places and people to your next level) are actually blocking you from those places and people (whether it be in family relationships, business relationships, professional relationships, social or spiritual relationships).

4. **CHOOSING BETWEEN BEING A VOICE OF WISDOM AND GUIDANCE AS A MENTOR OR A VOICE OF ONE WHO MISLEADS OUT OF NEGLECT**

You are DEFINED by choosing between a voice leading you to give your time and energy to offer wisdom and guidance as a mentor, coach etc. OR a voice leading you to neglect that role because it is too tedious and time consuming.

A **Destiny Connector** will embark on nurturing, mentoring, coaching and counselling her protégés intentionally and Purposefully with a lot of skill, care and Concern. She focuses on guiding them through difficult situation, rebuking them in love, pointing out the mine fields and dangers on the way etc. until they fulfil their Destiny and Purpose.

Whereas a **Destiny Blocker** will not be committed in her role but will be indifferent and negligent so that even when her assignees embark on a wrong decision and wrong directions, she does not seek to redirect them, or guard them from aborting their Purpose and Destiny.

"It is no profit to have learnt well, if you neglect to do well." ~ **Publilius Syrus**

A **Destiny Blocker** fails to hinder them from wrong relationships that draw them further away from their Purpose and Destiny. So, a **Destiny Blocker** is one who blocks the Destiny of others sometimes out of negligence and indifference than in what she actually does.

5. CHOOSING BETWEEN A VOICE OF HEALING FROM PAST PAIN OR A VOICE THAT HOLDS ON TO PAST PAIN

You are DEFINED by choosing between a voice leading you to embrace healing for your own past pain and struggles so that you can be effective in your connecting role OR a voice leading you to remain in your past pain as a victim and unable to play your proper connecting role.

"Healing may not be so much about getting better, as about letting go of everything that isn't you - all of the expectations, all of the beliefs and becoming who you are." ~ **Rachel Naomi Remen**

A **Destiny Connector** like Naomi is one who has probably encountered a lot of past pain and tragedy, failures and losses. Yet she still immerses herself selflessly into ensuring that her assignees fulfil and enter their Destiny. In the process of focusing on the welfare of others she gradually heals her own past pain and woundedness.

"It's never too early or too late to work towards being the healthiest you." ~ **Unknown**

Having agreed to play her role and usher her assignee to her Destiny, Naomi the connector helped her assignee to heal from her traumas and from her losses and in the process, the connector herself ultimately heals from her own losses and traumas.

"Do not remember the former things, nor consider the things of old. Behold, I will do a new thing, now it shall spring forth; shall you not know it? I will even make a road in the wilderness and rivers in the desert." **(Isa.43:18–19)**

Always listen to the voice encouraging you to seek healing for yourself and others instead of listening to the voice leading you to self- pity and a victim mentality.

6. CHOOSING BETWEEN A VOICE THAT SHEDS LIGHT AND TRUTH OR A VOICE THAT WITHHOLDS THE LIGHT AND THE TRUTH.

You are DEFINED by choosing between a voice that leads you to shed light and truth in a matter OR a voice leading you to withhold that light and truth in a matter.

"No amount of darkness can hide a spark of light." ~ **Unknown**

The **Destiny Connector** Naomi, was quick to shed light regarding the culture of a kinsman redeemer to her assignee so as to encourage her and boost her faith on the future.

The **Destiny Blocker** Rebecca, on the other hand when she saw that there had been confusion (where her blind husband could not differentiate between) she failed to shed light and truth in the matter which would have arrested the calamity that followed. She did not trust God enough to fulfil his promise so she interfered.

In your mandate of ushering others to their Destiny, you must ensure to bring clarity and truth to situations whenever you see that there is an absence of adequate information to enable them make informed decisions. Also, where you find that there has been a cloud of confusion, miscommunication and misunderstandings and you know that you are in a position to bring clarity to the situation.

"To give light to those who sit in darkness and the shadow of death, to guide our feet into the way of peace." **(Luke.1:79)**

You must also be one who stands for the truth, honesty and transparency in every situation. You should influence others to also adopt these principles because Destiny cannot be attained or fulfilled through darkness, confusion or deception.

You must therefore learn to heed to a voice telling you to walk in truth and clarity as opposed to listening to a voice telling you to use deceptive methods.

7. CHOOSING BETWEEN A VOICE THAT USHERS OTHERS TO DESTINY OR A VOICE THAT FOCUSES ONLY ON SELF

You are DEFINED by choosing between a voice leading you to usher others to Destiny OR a voice leading you to sit back and focus only on your own.

In the process of being consumed in ensuring that her assignees lay hold of their blessings and miracles a **Destiny Connector** lays hold of her own blessings and miracles. As a **Destiny Connector** ushers and propels others to enter their destinies and leave lasting legacies she herself finally enters her Destiny and leaves a lasting legacy.

A **Destiny Connector** understands that when she is ushering others to Destiny, it is always about them and not about her so she must suspend her own dysfunctions, hurts and pains long enough to finish her assignment concerning them and only then, will she herself be guaranteed of her own Destiny.

Naomi's obedience in ushering her assignee Ruth safely to her Destiny was the key to herself entering her own Destiny. Even as her assignee left a good legacy, so did she and even as the assignee was in the genealogy of Jesus, so was she.

The voice of a **Destiny Connector** tells you that ushering others to their Destiny is worth it no matter what sacrifices, sufferings and price you may have to pay. It is that selfless act that becomes a catalyst for you to also fulfil your own Destiny in the process and simultaneously.

Beware of listening to any other voice that tells you that you are being short-changed by using up all your time and energy in ushering others to their Destiny. Nor should you listen to that voice of fear telling you that you are wasting too much time serving others and that time may run out for you to focus on your own welfare. The selfless voice within you should always be louder than the selfish fearful voice within you.

Destiny Questions to Ponder On

1. *How can you ensure that you disclose relevant knowledge and information to your protégés in a timely and effective manner to avoid prejudicing their Destiny?*

2. *How can you ensure that you always instill faith and hope in your protégés instead of fear and doubt?*

3. *How can you ensure that you feed and sustain your protégé(s) valuable relationships instead of destroying them?*

4. *How can you ensure to be a diligent mentor who offers wisdom and guidance as opposed to one who is reckless and negligent?*

5. *Have you ever found yourself suffering from past pain and how did it affect your ability to usher your protégés to their Destiny?*

6. *Are there instances where you have withheld the light and truth in a situation concerning your protégés instead of shedding light and truth?*

7. *How can you avoid being more focused on yourself and being more focused on your protégés?*

This Page Was Intentionally Left Blank

Chapter Nine

THE GLOBAL DESTINY CARRIER OR THE LOCAL DESTINY CARRIER

Enlarging and Extending Your Sphere Of Influence

Chapter Preview

1. *A voice that empathizes and supports or a voice that condemns and shames others.*

2. *A voice of excellence or a voice of mediocrity.*

3. *A voice that breaks your barrenness or a voice that mocks your barrenness.*

4. *A voice that responds wisely to your mockers or a voice that reacts unwisely to your mockers.*

5. *A voice that leads you to the right people and place to break your barrenness or a voice that leads you to the wrong people and place that cannot break your barrenness.*

6. *A voice that leads you to greater impact or a voice that stifles your impact.*

7. *A voice that makes you remain humble after your barrenness is broken or a voice that makes you prideful.*

OPENING REMARKS

You are a well-connected Destiny carrier but the type of Destiny you are carrying will depend on the voices within and around you that you are listening to. A **Global Destiny Carrier** is one who carries a Destiny big enough to impact nations while a **Local Destiny Carrier** is one who carries a Destiny that has limited impact to her and her small circle of loved ones.

1. CHOOSING A VOICE THAT EMPATHIZES AND SUPPORTS OR A VOICE THAT CONDEMNS AND SHAMES OTHERS

You are DEFINED by choosing between a voice leading you to empathize, support and lift up others in their journey to Destiny OR the voice leading you to shame, condemn and pull them down.

"You can only understand people if you feel them in yourself." ~ **John Steinbeck**

A **Global Destiny Carrier** is one whose Purpose and Destiny transcends nations and has a wide-reaching impact and influence in transforming lives and nations so it is not limited to a locality.

A **Global Destiny Carrier** will often experience a long delay in birthing her Purpose because of its very greatness. As she waits in anguish to birth that Purpose somehow, she knows deep within her that it's only a delay not a denial and that she must first be prepared and equipped to carry the weight of that Destiny.

A **Global Destiny Carrier** also understands that the Destiny she births will not be about her and that it will be beyond her.

In her anguish and her waiting she gets a revelation that she must make a vow to ultimately allow that Purpose (once she births it) go out for the benefit of nations.

Whereas a **Local Destiny Carrier** is one who does not need to wait long to birth something because whatever she carries and births is of no serious consequence, impact or influence. It has a limited impact and influence only within a locality.

A **Local Destiny Carrier** is one who has refused to stretch and apply herself hard enough in order to carry a global Destiny and she becomes complacent and settles for less than she was created for. This makes her unfulfilled which makes her operate with a negative energy condemning and shaming those who are seeking to stretch and apply themselves to conceive a global Destiny.

The **Local Destiny Carrier** is misguided into thinking that she is better than others, because she conceived her Destiny quickly without much waiting (while the potential **Global Destiny Carrier** is still barren and still waiting to conceive her global Destiny).

The story of Hannah a **Global Destiny Carrier** and her co-wife Peninah a **Local Destiny Carrier** found in 1 Samuel demonstrates this point.

Both wives were connected to the same environment and the same husband yet one was barren and the other was not. This is a scenario we sometimes see in the market place where two women located and connected to the same environment, same set of circumstances and opportunities, yet one is climbing the ladder to success but the other one is not for no apparent reason.

It is never over until it is over, so do not be premature in your conclusions and judgments. Whether you are in a home and marriage setting like the two wives, or whether in an organization, business, profession etc. you may find yourself connected to other women who are thriving and succeeding while you appear seemingly stagnant and unproductive, or you could be one of the women thriving and succeeding ahead of others.

Peninah became fruitful and productive under the same atmosphere and environment but Hannah on the other hand remained unfruitful and unproductive for no apparent or tangible reason.

Peninah did not empathize with Hannah but chose to taunt and mock her and make her life unbearable thereby magnifying the stigma of barrenness that Hannah had already struggled with. Peninah was shallow and she believed that her success could only come by undermining and oppressing others.

Little did Peninah know that ultimately Hannah's barrenness would break and Hannah's seed would become more impactful than Peninah's seed.

A **Local Destiny Carrier** has a limited mentality. She is often misguided into thinking that her own success and achievements are determined by the failure of another one. So, she sets out to undermine as many as she can erroneously thinking that doing so will maintain her own success because she doesn't believe that there is room enough for all to succeed.

Whereas a **Global Destiny Carrier** celebrates the success and achievements of other women knowing that her own success thrives best among other success stories and that there is room for all of them to thrive and succeed. So, she sets out to pull up those who are down and to empathize with those in their dry and barren seasons. She wishes them well because she knows that seasons change and in her own season of dryness and barrenness, she will need the same empathy and pulling up.

Whether your barrenness is physical, financial, relational, spiritual or emotional etc. remember that, the seasons always change.

Always listen to the voice that tells you to empathize and lift others up in their down season because like a bicycle when one peddles is up the other one is down and there is no permanent season in any one 's life.

As a Woman of Destiny, you should empathize and lift up another Woman of Destiny during her season of barrenness, so that you can connect with the greatness within her, when her barrenness breaks.

2. CHOOSING A VOICE OF EXCELLENCE OR THE VOICE OF MEDIOCRITY

You are DEFINED by choosing between a voice leading you to become a high achiever OR a voice leading you to settle for mediocrity.

"We are what we repeatedly do. Excellence, then, is not an act, but a habit." **~ Will Durant**

A **Global Destiny Carrier** understands that in order to conceive and carry a Purpose that will impact nations, she must refuse to settle for less and choose to wait (no matter how long) for that which is excellent and that which she's been called for.

"Excellence is to do a common thing in an uncommon way." **~Booker T. Washington**

Even though she may be surrounded by mediocrity (especially those who love her and mean well but who cannot understand that which she's yearning for and they are constantly trying to convince her to settle for less) she must remain resilient and so focused in waiting for what she knows is her portion.

"As for the saints who are on the earth, 'They are the excellent ones, in whom is all my delight." **(Psalms.16:3)**

Whereas a **Local Destiny Carrier** will readily accept that which is less than what she is entitled to and she will settle in a place of mediocrity, insignificance and irrelevance never seeking to climb above her limitations.

"Don't waste your life. No one chooses mediocrity but many settle for it. Never settle." **~ Unknown**

You must adopt the attitude of a high achiever while fulfilling your Destiny. Resist any proposition to settle for less than that which you were born and created for nor should you agree to accept less than what you are entitled to.

Mediocrity should never be a word in your vocabulary because your Destiny requires a high level of excellence in fulfilling it. Do not resort to taking shortcuts or doing a half-hearted kid job just because you do not want to pay the price and make the sacrifices required.

Let it never be said about you that you were capable and had the potential to fulfil your Destiny at a higher level (that would have had greater impact) but that unfortunately you fell short.

The voice of a high achiever with excellence within you should always be louder than the voice of mediocrity.

3. CHOOSING A VOICE THAT BREAKS YOUR BARRENNESS OR A VOICE THAT MOCKS YOUR BARRENNESS

DEFINED by choosing between a voice that will lead you to focus and press into the breaker of your barrenness OR the voice that leads you to focus and listen to the mockers and sustainers of your barrenness.

A **Global Destiny Carrier** when in her seasons of barrenness, (whether it be physical, relational, emotional, financial, spiritual etc.) always knows the voice of the things, actions and people that can break her barrenness. So, she sets out to seek those things, take those actions and locate those people in order to break her barrenness.

More importantly, she knows the voice of the things, actions and people that will keep her in her barrenness like her mockers and the sustainers of her barrenness. She knows the need to disengage and disentangle herself from them in order to focus only on what will break her barrenness. (Disengaging and disentangling does not necessarily mean physically but it means mentally and emotionally because in the case of a husband and family members you may not be able to physically separate yourself from them).

Please note that a sustainer of your barrenness is more dangerous than a mocker of your barrenness. Sustainers of your barrenness are people who love you and mean you well but they do not have a revelation regarding the global Destiny that you are yearning to conceive and birth. So, as they watch you in your pain and barrenness, they are misguided into thinking that they can offer substitutes to replace that which you are hurting and yearning for.

To this extent they seek to sustain your barrenness by their sincere yet misguided advice to you.

The mockers are those who taunt you maliciously into hurting you to think that perhaps you must have done something wrong to cause and deserve your barrenness. While the sustainers of your barrenness are those people, who seek to convince you to forget that which you are desperately trying to conceive, birth or achieve and to settle for other lesser things and easier things. These are the two voices within and around you that you must silence completely, (keeping in mind that silencing these voices doesn't mean confronting these people and wasting a lot of time and energy on them but rather it means refusing to listen or to take in their negativity and misguided advice).

Peninah (the **Local Destiny Carrier**) sadly failed to understand that you may have a lot of seeds (meaning quantity) which may not bear significant fruit. Her many children did not become significant and impactful whereas Hannah's seed was quality (not quantity) and became very significant and impactful.

Your Destiny will require valuable relationships and connections. Understanding the role and value of each relationship and connection is key (and in this case) identifying and entrusting yourself into the hands of those who are equipped and empowered to break your barrenness is crucial and important.

Woe unto those who spend valuable time and energy connecting to those who are mockers and who have no power to break your barrenness. Let the voice of your barren breaker within you always be louder than the voice of your barren mocker or barren sustainer.

4. CHOOSING A VOICE THAT RESPONDS WISELY TO YOUR MOCKERS OR A VOICE THAT REACTS UNWISELY TO YOUR MOCKERS

You are DEFINED by choosing between a voice that helps you to see your mocker as a positive force that provokes you to Destiny OR a voice that misleads you to waste your valuable time and energy resenting your mockers.

A **Global Destiny Carrier** will have many mockers taunting her when she is still in the agony of her barrenness waiting to conceive her Purpose. Instead of focusing and wasting her energy on confronting and striving with her mockers, she chooses to redirect her focus and energy to seeking the one who can break her barrenness and locating the place where her barrenness will be broken.

"Don't waste your life. No one chooses mediocrity but many settle for it. Never settle." **Unknown**

A **Global Destiny Carrier** knows for sure that her mockers have no power to break her barrenness and to that extent they become irrelevant and insignificant in her game plan

"The mocker will not have the last laugh." **~Ravi Zacharias**

Whereas a **Local Destiny Carrier** in her misguided sense of self-importance will engage in taunting the **Global Destiny Carrier**s in their seasons of barrenness not knowing that every season has an end and that every captivity has a turn.

Fortunately, Hannah quickly realized that her mocker Peninah, was actually someone she could use to positively provoke her (into refusing to accept her barrenness and to push harder into having that barrenness broken). So, she chooses not to waste her energy reacting to her co-wife and instead she turns Peninah's negative force into a positive force for propelling her towards her miracle.

In your journey to Destiny your mockers will be many and your wisdom lies in understanding how to respond to them to your advantage as opposed to how to react to them to your disadvantage. Responding wisely is always more powerful than reacting.

The voice of the mocker around you should be specifically for Purposes of provoking you and challenging you to your Destiny but not for the Purposes of discouraging or derailing you.

5. **CHOOSING A VOICE THAT LEADS YOU TO THE RIGHT PEOPLE AND PLACE TO BREAKING YOUR BARRENNESS OR A VOICE THAT LEADS YOU TO THE WRONG PEOPLE AND PLACE**

You are DEFINED by choosing between a voice that will lead you to a place where your barrenness will be broken OR the voice that will lead you to remain in your place of barrenness.

A **Global Destiny Carrier** knows that apart from knowing that there are people, things and actions that will break her barrenness she also knows that there is a place where her barrenness will be broken. So, she embarks on seeking that place whether it be physical, mental, emotional, relational or spiritual etc. until she finds it.

This is because your barrenness in whichever area of your life it is, could be as a result of being in the wrong place (which is not your place of Purpose). Or it could be as a result of a mental or emotional bondage and mind-set or as a result of wrong relationships that you are yoked with or as a result of not walking right morally and spiritually. So, there must be a shift whether emotionally, mentally, physically, relationally or spiritually etc. for you to locate that place where barrenness will be broken.

It is a place where she must separate herself in deep worship and travail. She knows that it's her worship and travailing that will get her the attention of the breaker of her barrenness and it is what will provoke the breaker of her barrenness into action.

Whereas the **Local Destiny Carrier** does not realize that not all her barrenness has been broken and if only she could discover who can break that remaining barrenness, she would be able to become more fruitful and convert from being a **Local Destiny Carrier** into a **Global Destiny Carrier**.

Hannah the **Global Destiny Carrier** went to a place called "Shiloh" symbolizing a place of worship and intimacy with her God because she knew only God could break her barrenness.

For every problem and dilemma in your life there will always be a place where that dilemma and problem can be resolved and dealt with. It is therefore important for you to be alert and sensitive as to the places around you that have the answers and the solutions that you need.

There will be different places for the breaking of different types of barrenness within you. There will be a place of wealth for breaking your financial barrenness, a place of love and acceptance for breaking your emotional barrenness, a place of prayer for breaking your spiritual barrenness, a place of wisdom for breaking your mental and intellectual barrenness etc.

Within you there will be a voice leading you to the right places for the breaking of your barrenness whatever that barrenness may be. There will also be a voice misleading you to the wrong places where your barrenness cannot be broken and it will be up to you to decide which voice you will allow to be loudest in shaping you.

6. CHOOSING A VOICE THAT LEADS YOU TO GREATER IMPACT OR A VOICE THAT STIFLES YOUR IMPACT.

You are DEFINED by choosing between a voice that will lead you to wean and release your Destiny for global impact OR the voice leading you to hold on to that Destiny and keep it limited to you and your locality.

A **Global Destiny Carrier** remembers that her Purpose is for the benefit of others and not just for her own benefit. So as soon as she births it she knows that a season will come when she must wean it and release it selflessly by embracing people to benefit, partake and be part of it.

Whereas a **Local Destiny Carrier** has a narrow understanding of her Purpose so she holds on to it selfishly and builds her own self-centered kingdom around it so that it only benefits her and her inner circle. Therefore, it remains rooted and bound in its limited environment.

"Let nothing be done through selfish ambition or conceit, but in lowliness of mind let each esteem others better than himself. Let each of you look out not only for his own interests, but also for the interests of others." **(Phil 2:3-4)**

A **Global Destiny Carrier** allows her Purpose to break barriers and all limitations to impact future generations because it leaves a positive legacy and has a far-reaching influence.

Whereas a **Local Destiny Carrier** is content in having her Purpose remain grounded and rooted in limitations without breaking any barriers or going above its limitations and without leaving a worthwhile legacy for the future generations.

Peninah the **Local Destiny Carrier** was one who focused on the wrong things, wrong places and wrong people. In the process her seed did not cause any impact or any influence or any positive transformation to her generation, society and nation.

She sadly dies in oblivion and obscurity and chances are that, had she empathized with (instead of mocking) her co-wife, chances are she would have had an opportunity to play a positive role in breaking her co-wife's barrenness and in ushering her into her Destiny, and in so doing entering her own Destiny as a **Global Destiny Carrier** instead of remaining as a **Local Destiny Carrier**.

For every Woman in the market place today, this is a crucial lesson, our own success will come by helping others to succeed and our own empowerment will only come by empowering others.

"An empowered Woman empowers" **~Unknown**

We also learn that in our journey to Destiny we will encounter all manner of distractions and attempts to derail us especially by poisoning our souls and minds, so that we become wounded and bitter resentful and offended. All this toxic baggage only slows down our progress and journey.

Hannah the **Global Destiny Carrier** understood that the seed of greatness she was ordained to conceive, carry and bring forth would take time, patience, trust and faith because of the great impact it would ultimately have.

Her barrenness was finally broken because she directed her focus in the right place, in the right things and action and on the right people and she brought forth fruit that ended up impacting and transforming her generation, her society and her nation.

Beware of a voice that seeks to influence you to make your Destiny about yourself and not about others. Beware of a voice that keeps telling you that you have suffered too much and for too long and that you have paid such a high price. This voice therefore misleads you that you should be the only beneficiary of your Purpose and Destiny. You must resist that voice and choose the voice that constantly reminds you that your Purpose and Destiny were never about benefiting you alone but about benefiting others first.

7. CHOOSING A VOICE THAT MAKES YOU REMAIN HUMBLE AFTER YOUR BARRENNESS IS BROKEN OR A VOICE THAT MAKES YOU PRIDEFUL

You are DEFINED by choosing between a voice telling you to be humble and grateful when your barrenness is broken OR a voice telling you to show off, boast and revenge against those who mocked you.

The **Global Destiny Carrier** is a true Woman of Destiny who understands the grace and favour it took to break her barrenness. So that when her barrenness is broken and she brings forth, she does not focus on boasting and showing off to those who mocked her, like many would be tempted to do. Instead, she understands the need to express deep gratitude to those that had helped her break her barrenness.

Hannah had matured so much during her seasons of barrenness and travail that every shallow pettiness and desire to prove herself had died within her and she now arose as a victorious Woman without any grudges or bitterness against her mocker and instead Hannah sang a song of praise to God (1 Samuel Chapter 2).

Indeed, it is often when we are not yet delivered from pettiness, bitterness and the need to prove ourselves to others that we delay the breaking of our barrenness in the various areas of our lives. It is only when we have come to a place of maturity and died to our flesh and carnal habits and behaviours that our barrenness is broken and we lay hold of that which we have been travailing for.

In fact, you have more power to positively transform those who have mocked you in your season of barrenness when they marvel at your beautiful, mature attitude once your barrenness is broken as opposed to turning yourself into a mocker like them.

Let the voice of gratitude, grace and forbearance within you speak louder than the voice that seeks to boast, show off and revenge.

Destiny Questions to Ponder On

1. *In what other ways can you ensure that you remain emphatic and supportive of others in their seasons of suffering?*

2. *What other factors can help you become a high achiever?*

3. *How do you locate the breakers of your barrenness?*

4. *Why is it important to respond to your mockers positively instead of reacting negatively?*

5. *How do you recognize the right place for breaking your barrenness?*

6. *How do you handle the sustainers of your barrenness?*

7. *How can you ensure to remain humble after your barrenness is broken?*

This Page Was Intentionally Left Blank

Chapter Ten

THE DESTINY RESPECTER OR THE DESTINY DESPISER

Moving From A Place Of Tolerance To A Place Of Celebration

Chapter Preview

1. *A voice that discerns defining moments or a voice that misses defining moments.*

2. *A voice that helps you transition towards Destiny or a voice that hinders your transition.*

3. *A voice of love and acceptance or a voice of pain and abandonment.*

4. *A voice that embraces new systems and new ways of thinking or a voice that sticks to old systems and old ways of thinking.*

5. *A voice that connects to valuable relationships or a voice that disconnects from such relationships.*

6. *A voice that embraces the power of choice or a voice that remains powerless.*

7. *A voice that speaks of vibrant dreams or a voice that speaks of shattered dreams.*

OPENING REMARKS

How you move towards your Destiny will reveal whether you are one who respects Destiny or one who despises Destiny. More so, your respecting or despising will have been as a result of the voices within and around you that you have chosen to listen to.

To **respect** Destiny is to put value on it and to give it priority and to be ready to make whatever sacrifices and bear whatever pain you need to bear and incur whatever costs you may need to incur or pay whatever price you need to pay in order to live out and fulfil your Destiny. It means that you care deeply for your Destiny and the Destiny of others.

Whereas to **despise** Destiny is to dishonour it, relegate it as a last priority in your life and as a non-consequence and to make it quite clear that you are not willing to pay any price, incur any cost, make any sacrifices or bear any pain in order to live it out and fulfil it.

It means that you do not care about your Destiny or the Destiny of others.

1. CHOOSING BETWEEN A VOICE THAT DISCERNS DEFINING MOMENTS OR A VOICE THAT MISSES DEFINING MOMENTS

You are DEFINED by choosing between a voice that will lead you to discern defining moments for making your Destiny moves OR a voice that will lead you to missing those defining moments and thereby you fail to make your Destiny moves.

A **respecter of Destiny** is one who has some revelation about Destiny and she initially finds herself in a pathetic environment (whether it be a relationship, a career, a business enterprise, a church ministry, an institution or an organization) where she is not fulfilling her Purpose and no one else in that environment seems to have any revelation about Destiny. Yet deep within her there is a yearning and a desire for better and more even though she cannot quite put her finger on what that better and more is.

To others in that environment, her emptiness and restlessness may seem vain because in their view she has everything that they think she could possibly want or need in terms of material substance and social status.

But it is that yearning and emptiness within her that enables her to recognize an hour of visitation when an opportunity presents itself. She is able to confirm in her heart that this is the opportunity she has been waiting for in order to relocate from her Destiny-less environment (where there is no Vision and the people keep perishing) to a place of Destiny.

A respecter of Destiny understands the need to wait patiently for the right timing instead of seeking to make a move at the wrong time. When making a Destiny move timing is everything because any attempt to move at the wrong time you will find yourself caught between the place of distress and the place of Destiny (which is a place of confusion).

On the other hand, a **despiser of Destiny** is one who is content in an environment and among people where Destiny and Purpose are not a priority. She simply enjoys the luxuries, social status and material comforts that come with her environment simply because she does not know that there is anything better beyond where she is at. So even where an opportunity comes when she could move from that place of distress to a place of Destiny she is not alert or sensitive enough to recognize it and step into it consciously.

Sometimes those around a despiser of Destiny may accidentally subconsciously push her into a place where there is potential for her to fulfil Destiny. They do so (not because they want her to fulfil any Destiny) but because she is a pawn in their hands and under their control to serve their own interests.

Unfortunately, when a **Destiny Despiser** is pushed into that place of Destiny, she does not even recognize or discern it. So, she tragically fails to connect to that place of Destiny. She more or less remains in a paradoxical state in the sense that she is in a place of Destiny externally but she remains in a place of distress internally.

A **Destiny Despiser** therefore is one who is emotionally in the place of distress but physically in the place of Destiny, which ultimately causes her to disintegrate and rip apart to her destruction because of the conflict within her.

There are two women in the bible one called Abigail, the wife of Nabal (1 Samuel 20) and the other called Michal, the daughter of King Saul (1 Samuel 25) who both became David's wives at different times and under different circumstances.

Abigail had been married to Nabal, a wealthy man who loved his drink and who was not very wise, and we know she was an intelligent Woman full of wisdom (so by implication her marriage to Nabal must have been an emotional distress and a gross mismatch).

When the reckless and arrogant behaviour of her husband Nabal made him insult David and his men, she knew David could have easily destroyed them (which would have caused David to have unnecessary blood on his hands). So, in her wisdom she did some damage control and appeased the situation. She had a revelation that David was a Destiny carrier so her wise action safeguarded his honour and reputation.

Abigail saw her hour of visitation when David offered to marry her following her husband's death and she stepped into her defining moment to connect with David. Her decision to connect to David symbolized a decision to connect to Destiny and in doing so, she relocated from a place of distress to a place of Destiny. Abigail was a respecter of Destiny and her radical and wise decision secured her own Destiny while safeguarding David's.

Whenever you are stuck and internally conflicted between places and choices and when you fail to make up your mind, the consequences are that you will be destroyed at the place of your conflict because the conflict itself will rip you apart.

Within you there will always be a voice that provokes and encourages you to move away from your place of distress into your place of Destiny. Yet there will also be a voice that seeks to convince you that you are not in a place of distress or that the distress is not that bad and that you should settle there since the price for moving away may be too high.

However, Michal, who was given to David as a trophy for winning a battle initially loved and protected David especially at one time when her father King Saul sought to kill David. However, many years later she came to despise him. Ironically, she loved and protected him in the days when he was not yet great but she despised him later on when he was in the centre of fulfilling his Destiny and he had become a force to reckon with and greater than her own father King Saul.

This seems to imply that either Michal had never understood David's Destiny at all from the beginning or the years of separation from David had made her bitter and disillusioned. Suffice to say she stands out as a despiser of Destiny who sadly failed to see her defining moment and relocate from her place of distress to her place of Destiny. So that even though she was in a place of Destiny as David's wife, (surrounded by Destiny unfolding) she however emotionally remained in her place of distress too bitter to make the crucial shift and transition.

One of the most important things in your journey to Destiny will be to discern your defining moments and hours of visitation and to take the necessary radical action in the proper timing in order to move on to your next level in fulfilling your Destiny.

2. CHOOSING BETWEEN A VOICE THAT HELPS YOU TRANSITION OR A VOICE THAT HINDERS YOUR TRANSITION

You are DEFINED by choosing between a voice that will help you to transition OR a voice that will discourage you from transitioning.

A **Destiny Respecter** is one who finds herself in an environment (whether a business, career, relationship etc.) where despite the material comforts and social status, deep down she knows that she is an insignificant element in that environment and that it will eventually suffocate her.

She knows that her role there does not make or break anything of significance. Her opinions and views are not taken seriously and she is more or less seen as a benefactor of that environment as opposed to being seen as a valuable contributor to that environment.

"What a man does for pay is of little significance. What he is, as a sensitive instrument responsive to the world's beauty, is everything." ~ **H. P. Lovecraft**

Deep down Abigail knew that she could be significant and relevant in some other environment and hence her daily desire and dream to find that significant place.

So, when her opportunity to step into significance presents itself, she is so ready and nothing can hold her back.

"What will matter is not your success but your significance." ~ **Michael Josephson**

Whereas Michal, the **Destiny Despiser**, was a pawn in her father's palace waiting to be given to the highest bidder without a say, (showing that she was dispensable to her father and family). So perhaps the more reason she should have recognized and appreciated the change from a place of distress where she had no voice and no value to a place of Destiny as David's wife where she would help him fulfil Destiny and in so doing fulfil her own but sadly Michal never got this revelation.

Both women got a chance to become relevant and significant with King David and to partake in his successes and victories, but while the **Destiny Respecter** appreciated that shift and thrived in it, the **Destiny Despiser** eventually resented it and dried up in it.

A **Destiny Despiser** does not have any clue about her insignificance in her place of distress. She is so lethargic in her mundane and meaningless existence which has become acceptable to her. In addition, she may also be content with her social status and allow it to define her and fulfil her even though that fulfilment is hollow.

Thus, even when she is presented with an opportunity to move from insignificance to significance, a **Destiny Despiser** does not take it because she does not know that she is not significant thereby missing a chance to fulfil Destiny.

The voice within you that desires to propel you to places of significance must always be louder than the voice within you that convinces you that you are okay where you are.

3. CHOOSING BETWEEN A VOICE OF LOVE AND ACCEPTANCE OR A VOICE OF PAIN AND ABANDONMENT

You are DEFINED by choosing between a voice that will lead you to embrace your place of love and acceptance OR a voice that will lead you to remain in your place of pain and abandonment.

A **Destiny Respecter** is one who finds herself in a place of emotional abuse where the abuse is so subtle that those around her cannot perceive it and those causing her the abuse do not know that they are causing her abuse.

This is the most frustrating type of abuse because often you are the only one who can discern it which means that you do not get support from those, you'd expect to get support from in addressing and confronting that abuse.

A subtle abuse can be where those you are connected to are living and behaving in a manner that causes you distress and repulsion even though they are not forcing you to partake in their behaviour and lifestyle. Nonetheless, you are so closely connected to them that day in and day out, you are suffocated and immersed in their toxic behaviour and lifestyle. This can justifiably be deemed as a form of emotional abuse. This appears to have been Abigail's distress.

Having endured this kind of abuse over a long period of time, a **Destiny Respecter** is eager to embrace a place of love and acceptance when it presents itself. She doesn't take it for granted and embraces it wholeheartedly Purposefully and intentionally expediting healing from her past pain and wounds.

One of the differences between a respecter of Destiny and despiser of Destiny is that a respecter's yearning to lock into her own Destiny makes her stronger in climbing out of the pit of abusive relationships and toxic environments. Her Destiny cries out so powerfully within her that it empowers her to reject every form of abuse that is threatening to stifle and kill her Destiny. So, her passion for Destiny protects and preserves her.

Whereas a despiser of Destiny has nothing with which to repel the abuse. She doesn't have the power and passion for Destiny within her to fight and climb out of the pits of abuse so she normalizes it in order to live with it.

The respecter of Destiny easily moves to a place of love and acceptance because she knows that her Destiny will feed and thrive in such a place. The despiser of Destiny has no Destiny to feed so she remains in the place without love and acceptance.

In your journey to Destiny, you must be eager and quick to move out of a place where you have no love and acceptance and move to a place where you will find love and acceptance. A place where you will be valued and celebrated in order to fulfil your Destiny.

Abigail the **Destiny Respecter** was able to heal and leave her woundedness behind but Michal, the **Destiny Despiser** was not able to and, in the end, her woundedness gave birth to dishonour and disloyalty that caused her to despise her husband King David.

Your past pain and woundedness will always become a pitfall in your journey to Destiny, so you must get over it. Your ability to let go and heal is one of the most powerful Destiny choices you will ever make.

It is so sad that within most women there is often a nasty voice that seeks to convince you to normalize the abuse in your life or to convince you that you are to blame for that abuse and that therefore you should not seek to come out of it. However, you must radically arise and choose to listen to the voice within you telling you that you were not born or created to be abused, mishandled or mistreated. Listen to the voice that says you are precious and valuable. Allowing abuse in your life will seriously hinder you from fulfilling your Destiny.

4. CHOOSING BETWEEN A VOICE THAT EMBRACES NEW SYSTEMS AND WAYS OF THINKING OR A VOICE THAT STICKS TO OLD SYSTEMS AND OLD WAYS OF THINKING

DEFINED by choosing between a voice that will lead you to embrace new systems and ways of thinking OR a voice leading you to remain in old systems and ways of thinking.

A **Destiny Respecter** is one who initially finds herself in an old dispensation where everything is outdated and there is no longer new Vision, no new ideas. The pace of productivity or fruitfulness around her is slow if at all, and things the people hold dear have been overtaken and are no longer relevant or valuable.

Somehow, she knows that there is another place where there is a new dispensation with a new move where the ideas are fresh and innovative and where there is fruitfulness and productivity and where the atmosphere and climate is favourable and conducive to fulfil Destiny.

A **Destiny Respecter** seeks every opportunity to disconnect from the old dispensation into the new dispensation. However, a **Destiny Despiser** is so oblivious of the value of Destiny that she remains content with the outdated and stale ideas, retrogressive mind-sets, and stagnancy.

In the event that somehow, she does get pushed into a new dispensation, she fails to connect to it and even though she remains in that new dispensation, she despises it and fails to thrive in it and ultimately dies in it barren.

The despiser found herself privileged to be connected to the right and influential people without even knowing and if she knew it, she failed to perceive the need to tap into that greatness and therefore fails to reap from it.

In your journey to Destiny, there will be key people/ relationships that you will need to recognize as your **Destiny Connector**s, so that you sow into the hidden yet unleashed greatness within them for a future harvest.

The **Destiny Respecter** recognized the people who mattered and honoured and respected them and connected to them knowing that it was to her benefit for fulfilling her Purpose and Destiny.

She had a clear revelation of who the man of Destiny was in the scheme of things and the greatness that lay within him (even though he was not yet king but still a fugitive). She knew that connecting to him and sowing into his Purpose would guarantee her own Purpose and Destiny.

Both King Saul and Nabal represented the old and rejected on their way out, while David represented the new and accepted on their way in. In our journey to Destiny and in our careers, Callings, relationships, parenting, businesses etc. we must constantly be alert as agents of positive change to recognize those ideas, strategies, mind-sets that are old and distorted and align ourselves with innovative new ways of thinking and working in order to remain on the cutting edge.

As a Woman of Destiny, you must accept change, new ideas and innovation as you fulfil your Destiny. You must be able to recognize the old that is being replaced by the new whether it be old priesthoods, old dispensations, old ways of thinking and doing things because you must embrace progress that is positive and Destiny enhancing.

The voice within you that resists change will always hold you back from effectively and progressively moving to your Destiny so you must choose to listen to the voice that encourages you to accept positive change which will propel you to your Destiny.

5. CHOOSING BETWEEN A VOICE THAT CONNECTS TO VALUABLE RELATIONSHIPS OR A VOICE THAT DISCONNECTS FROM SUCH RELATIONSHIPS

You are DEFINED by choosing between a voice that leads you to connect with meaningful valuable relationships OR a voice that leads you to disconnect with such relationships.

"Blessed is the man who walks not in the counsel of the ungodly, nor stands in the path of sinners, nor sits in the seat of the scornful." **(Psalm.1:1)**

A **Destiny Respecter** is one who finds herself connected to valuable of relationships because of her thirst and hunger to discover and fulfil her Destiny. She has the revelation that one of the most fundamental and necessary tools for fulfilling her Purpose and Destiny is relationships. She skillfully begins to sieve and sift the relationships around her disconnecting from the carnal time-wasting toxic relationships and connecting to the valuable and healthy relationships.

"A healthy relationship doesn't drag down; it inspires you to better."
~ Mandy Hale

She learns to differentiate between those around her who are focused on that which is carnal and fleshly and temporal and those who are focused on that which is divine and eternal.

"You are allowed to terminate toxic relationships; you are allowed to walk away from people who hurt you. You are allowed to be angry; you don't owe anyone an explanation for taking care of yourself." ~ **Unknown**

The **Destiny Respecter** is acutely **aware** that relationships and associations define her and they either add to or deduct from the capacity within her to fulfil her Purposes and Destiny.

Whereas a **Destiny Despiser** having no revelation about her Purpose and Destiny (or where she has a revelation, she puts no value to her Purpose and Destiny), fails to distinguish between the relationships around her whereby those that would have propelled her to her Destiny melt away because they are not appreciated and valued.

She ends up with the meaningless toxic relationships that will never usher her to her Destiny and if by any stroke of luck, she finds herself in a valuable Destiny propelling relationship, she sabotages it because she looks at it superficially and despises it probably because she cannot see the hidden potential and greatness in that relationship.

In the long run she loses that relationship and she dies barren without ever having fulfilled her Destiny.

Abigail the **Destiny Respecter** connected to the man of Destiny and she became a great support to him and ended up benefitting her generation and nation. In the process of doing so she disconnected and got delivered from her pathetic circumstances and toxic connections.

However, Michal, the despiser of Destiny remained barren because of despising the man of Destiny and in the process, she never discovered and never fulfilled her Destiny.

Relationships have a lot to do with emotions, the voice within you misleading you to emotionally hold on to dead, toxic and fruitless relationships seems to always be louder than the voice that sternly and firmly warns you to disconnect and cut off all such relationships that hinder you from fulfilling your Destiny.

Fulfilling your Destiny will require the most radical choices and decisions that may not always be comfortable and in fact many of them will be very painful and distressful.

6. CHOOSING BETWEEN THE VOICE THAT EMBRACES THE POWER OF CHOICE OR A VOICE THAT REMAINS POWERLESS.

You are DEFINED by choosing between a voice leading you to embrace the power of choice and to master your own Destiny OR a voice leading you to allow others to take charge over you and master your Destiny.

A **Destiny Respecter** is one who finds herself in a place where she is yoked to an environment and relationships, where she is not a free agent to make her own choices and decisions nor set and determine the course of her life.

To that extent she lives as an appendix or addendum of that place and those relationships with no capacity to ever discover or fulfil her Destiny and Purpose. She is at a state of captivity until she makes a choice to move from captivity to freedom and she becomes a **Destiny Respecter**.

"There is no sorrow except in captivity." ~ **Rajneesh**

Whereas a **Destiny Despiser** is one who does not understand that her environment of hollow luxury and comfort is a bondage and captivity (where she is used as a pawn to fulfil other people's agendas) without being able to exercise any free choices of her own.

To that extent, she fails to make a move from that place of bondage and captivity, and even where she might find herself having escaped that place of bondage and captivity for some reason or other, she nonetheless fails to realize that she is in a place of liberty and free choice. She therefore remains passive paradoxically and physically in a place of liberty and free choice yet as a captive in bondage emotionally.

Michal, the **Destiny Despiser**'s lack of revelation about her own Purpose caused her to despise and disrespect David's passion for his Purpose and Destiny. Whereas Abigail the **Destiny Respecter** had a revelation about David's Destiny so she was able to respect it.

Both women had been in some kind of bondage but while the respecter easily adopted her new identity and shed off the tight garments of her former self, the **Destiny Despiser** remained clad in her former non-descript identity defined by the men that used her like a merchandise.

Becoming the captain and master of your Destiny is key to your ability in fulfilling it and consequently any sign of bondage in your life (whether internally or externally inflicted) will hinder and hamper you greatly in making free choices and decisions that are not tainted with other people's opinions and projections.

7. CHOOSING BETWEEN A VOICE THAT SPEAKS OF VIBRANT DREAMS OR A VOICE THAT SPEAKS OF SHATTERED DREAMS

DEFINED by choosing between a voice leading you to move from the place of your shattered dreams to a place where your dreams can shout again OR a voice leading you to remain in that place of dead dreams.

Every Woman has dreams regarding the various areas of her life whether it be family, career, business etc.

A **Destiny Respecter** is a Woman who harbours Destiny dreams and yearns for the fulfilment of those dreams but she finds herself in a place and environment where such dreams are suffocated and shattered. She lacks some fundamental tools to turn those dreams into reality such as Destiny connecting relationships in the form of midwives, mentors etc. because she is in an environment where there is no revelation of Destiny among the inhabitants.

It is a place full of dream killers, dream destroyers etc. and she relocates to a place where her dreams will be nurtured to manifest into reality and where she can fulfil her Purpose and Destiny.

Whereas a **Destiny Despiser** allows her environment and atmosphere (where there is no Vision and revelation of Destiny) to silence her and to steal any dreams she might have had.

Even when an opportunity arises where she can dream and fulfil her Purpose and Destiny, she enters that place but fails to connect to the dreamers there. If only she could connect to that place and to the people there, she would become ignited and be able to dream again, and have people with whom she can share her dreams and even actualize her dreams into reality.

Often, we reject second chances out of the fear of believing and trusting in something or someone again, for fear that we might be hurt and disappointed again.

Destiny is all about dreams and Visions so you should not listen to the voice that kills dreams and Visions. Instead, you should listen to the voice that fuels and ignites them.

Destiny Questions to Ponder On

1. *How do you discern defining moments?*

2. *What hinders you from transitioning?*

3. *What holds you back from accepting love and acceptance?*

4. *What makes you hold on to old systems and ways of thinking?*

5. *How do you connect to valuable relationships?*

6. *How do you embrace the power of choice?*

7. *How do you revive your shattered dreams?*

This Page Was Intentionally Left Blank

Chapter Eleven

THE EAGLE DESTINY OR THE CHICKEN DESTINY

Reaching For The Higher Things Of Life

Chapter Preview

1. *A voice hungry for higher things or a voice satisfied with lower things.*

2. *A voice to soar high or a voice to remain grounded.*

3. *A voice that thirsts for what quenches or a voice that has no thirst*

4. *A voice that defines you by who you were born to be or a voice that defines you by mundane things.*

5. *A voice that yearns for empowerment or a voice that yawns in apathy and indifference.*

6. *A voice that harnesses your focus and energy or a voice that misdirects that focus and energy.*

7. *A voice leading you to look up or a voice leading you to look down*

OPENING REMARKS

Ultimately you will be conflicted as regards whether to fulfil an **Eagle Destiny** or a **Chicken Destiny**. The determining factor will be the voices within and around you that you will have chosen to listen to. An **Eagle Destiny** is one that soars above to great heights whereas a **Chicken Destiny** is one that remains limited unable to quite take off from the ground.

"All birds find shelter during rain, but eagles avoid rain by flying above the Clouds" ~ **A. P. J. Abdul Kalam**

1. CHOOSING A VOICE THAT IS HUNGRY FOR THE HIGHER OR A VOICE THAT IS SATISFIED WITH THE LOWER

You are DEFINED by choosing between a voice telling you to hunger for deeper and higher things OR a voice telling you to be satisfied with shallow and base things.

An **Eagle Destiny** is one who knows the right things to feed herself with that will equip and empower her for Purposes of fulfilling her Purpose and Destiny. It is knowing the difference between feeding on what grows you and feeding on what stunts your growth.

She focuses her time and energy on things that are related to her Purpose and Destiny so she hungers for that which is uncommon and valuable and always seeks to see the depth of a matter.

She feeds on all things authentic because she knows authenticity is what will give her effectiveness. She therefore feeds her mind, body, soul and spirit.

Whereas a **Chicken Destiny** chooses to feed and dwell on the mundane things of life which stunt her growth because she fails to understand the difference between what matters and what does not and therefore, she conforms to what is shallow and common.

She focuses on feeding her body and fails to feed her mind, soul and spirit.

There is a story in the bible (Luke 10) of a set of sisters who were presented with the things that matter and things that do not matter in life. The first Woman, Mary (the eagle) chose the things that really matter, so she put her time and energy on those things. The 'eagle' hungers and thirsts for the uncommon, the hidden treasure that has real value.

Then there is the other sister, Martha the (chicken) who had the opportunity to place value on the right things but failed to do so. She chose to dwell on the mundane things in life and failed to see what really matters.

The 'eagle' was the one who chose to fly high above the norm and reached for that which is precious and rare and she chose to dwell high above the petty human negativity.

The 'chicken' chose to dwell down below in the midst of the human negative activities.

Your ability to fulfil your Destiny will always be measured by your hunger and more importantly your hunger for the right and valuable things that pertain to your Destiny.

Mary the **Eagle Destiny** carrier chose to sit at the feet of Jesus and soak in the deep and higher eternal things that Jesus was teaching that fed her spirit and pertained to Destiny, while Martha chose to busy herself with basic chores that would only feed the body but not the spirit, meaning that she chose the common and base things of this world while Mary chose the uncommon and eternal things.

So, there will be a voice that seeks to suppress that hunger for that which you need for your Destiny and instead it seeks to lead you to hunger for things contrary or not useful to your Destiny. It is this voice that you must ignore and instead listen to the voice that constantly reminds you to be hungry and never to get satisfied until you have fed yourself on those deeper and higher things that nourish you for Destiny.

2. CHOOSING A VOICE TO SOAR HIGH OR A VOICE TO REMAIN GROUNDED

You are DEFINED by choosing between a voice telling you to soar the sky like an eagle OR a voice telling you to scratch the ground like a chicken.

For an **Eagle Destiny**, even the skies are never the limit as she looks upwards and seeks to soar high above to reach upwards for things that are better and more excellent, things that will make her Purpose have more impact and influence. It is knowing the difference between choosing to fly high without limitations and choosing to remain limited and held down.

An **Eagle Destiny** rises above the petty human negativities of strife and gossip on the polluted ground because her focus is on things that are purifying and empowering and uplifting.

Whereas a **Chicken Destiny** chooses to dwell down below weighed down by the limitations and burdens of life with her face looking downwards at the cares and chores of daily life.

A **Chicken Destiny** remains ensnared with the base and polluted things on the ground which weaken and hinder her from fulfilling her Purpose and Destiny.

There will always be a voice of fear within you that causes you to fear to rise up and soar and unleash the potential within you. That voice fills you with fear that you are not capable of soaring higher than where you are and that you should therefore remain where you are on the ground where it is safer. You must reject that voice and choose to listen to the voice of the eagle within you that provokes and challenges you to rise above every limitation and obstacle in your life where even the sky cannot limit you.

3. CHOOSING A VOICE THAT THIRSTS FOR WHAT QUENCHES OR A VOICE THAT HAS NO THIRST

You are DEFINED by choosing between a voice telling you to thirst for that which really quenches OR a voice telling you to thirst for that which does not really quench.

An **Eagle Destiny** is one whose thirst can only be quenched by the fulfilment of her Purpose and Destiny so she chooses to drink from deep wells.

A **Chicken Destiny** is one whose thirst is easily quenched from shallow waters and she thirsts for that which does not really quench and therefore remains on the threshold of her Destiny having failed to fulfil her Purpose.

Mary the **Eagle Destiny** carrier ignored the mundane things of life because she had a deeper hunger for what truly matters while Martha the **Chicken Destiny** carrier remained thirsty and unquenched by the daily cares of life.

The voice within you that guides you towards the right wells where you will truly quench your thirst and be adequately hydrated for Destiny is the voice you must listen to. This is as opposed to the voice that leads you to the wrong wells that are dry or polluted and that never quite quench your thirst leaving you dehydrated and unable to fulfil your Destiny.

4. CHOOSING A VOICE THAT DEFINES YOU BY WHO YOU WERE BORN TO BE OR A VOICE DEFINED BY MUNDANE THINGS

DEFINED by choosing between a voice telling you to be defined by who you were born to be OR a voice telling you to be defined by the mundane things you do.

An **Eagle Destiny** is one whose self-identity is rooted in the things that matter and that are eternal, and that impact on her Purpose and Destiny.

"It's not what's happening to you now or what has happened in your past that determines who you become. Rather, it's your decisions about what to focus on, what things mean to you, and what you're going to do about them that will determine your ultimate Destiny." **~ Tony Robbins**

A **Chicken Destiny**'s identity is rooted in temporal transient things that do not speak to her Purpose and Destiny.

In this day and age when many are obsessed with titles and positions, power and success, it is very easy for you to be tempted to define yourself according to your high position in the marketplace (church, family or social standing) and to erroneously believe that those titles and positions are adequate in defining you. Yet to allow that to define you is to seriously short-change yourself because you are much more than that.

It is crucial that as you journey to Destiny you get a clear understanding of your identity and be secure in it and to clearly know what are the fundamentals that should define you (such as your choices, your voice, your Purpose, your hallmarks etc.). So that whenever there is a temptation to define yourself with the wrong things, then you can quickly arrest yourself. Mary the **Eagle Destiny** carrier chose to be defined by the word that was coming out of the mouth of the Lord that told her who she was and why she was created whereas Martha chose to be defined by the activities she was engaged in.

The voice within you seeking to make you become satisfied and be defined by positions and titles must never drown out the voice within you that tells you that you are much more than your activities, titles and positions.

5. CHOOSING A VOICE THAT YEARNS FOR EMPOWERMENT OR A VOICE THAT YAWNS IN APATHY AND INDIFFERENCE

You are DEFINED by choosing between a voice leading you to yearn for impartation and empowerment OR a voice leading you to yawn in apathy and indifference.

"For I long to see you, that I may impart to you some spiritual gift, so that you may be established." **(Rom 1:11)**

An **Eagle Destiny** feels restless and empty and therefore seeks to be imparted with things that will empower and equip her to fulfil her Purpose and enter Destiny.

"Empowerment is still one of the most important and powerful fundamental in the world building process that is born in mind first and then finds its reflection in different aspects of it." **~ Unknown**

A **Chicken Destiny** has no yearning and remains content with the emptiness within her thereby failing to fulfil her Purpose and Destiny.

You must resist the voice within you that always portrays you as a victim and instead listen to the voice within you that tells you are a victor because of your constant desire of greater impartation and empowerment.

6. CHOOSING A VOICE THAT HARNESSES YOUR FOCUS AND ENERGY OR A VOICE THAT MISDIRECTS THAT FOCUS AND ENERGY

You are DEFINED by choosing between a voice leading you to harness of focused energy within you OR a voice leading you to misdirect that focus and energy.

"Like a laser beam, focused energy is power. Don't let distractions weaken you." ~ **Unknown**

An **Eagle Destiny** is one who knows where to direct her energy and focus.

"Always remember, your focus determines your reality." ~ **George Lucas**

She knows the difference between the real issues and the non-issues, the fundamentals and the non-essentials so she side-lines anything that will drain her energy and attention so as to immerse herself completely in the fulfilment of her Purpose and Destiny.

Mary the **Eagle Destiny** carrier focused her energy in the right direction towards people and things that were eternal whereas Martha the **Chicken Destiny** carrier focused her energy on things and people that were temporary and mundane.

The voice that encourages you and energizes you is the voice that you must heed to as opposed to the voice that feeds you with negativity and discouragement and totally depletes you of your energy or misleads you to focus on the wrong things.

7. CHOOSING A VOICE LEADING YOU TO LOOK UP OR A VOICE LEADING YOU TO LOOK DOWN

You are DEFINED by choosing between a voice leading you to look up and take in the fresh air above OR a voice leading you to look down and take in the polluted stale air below.

An **Eagle Destiny** understands that only that which is fresh, new and innovative can propel her to her Destiny. So, she chooses to rise above in search of those things that are revolutionary, refreshing and innovative in order to be in sync with the times and seasons and in order to be at the cutting edge in her space. It is the difference between being propelled upwards by the fresh wind or being suffocated downwards by the polluted stale wind.

"By all means never fail to get all the sunshine and fresh air you can."
~ Joseph Pilates

Whereas a **Chicken Destiny** by choosing to remain bowed down in the old and outdated things, ends up becoming polluted by the stale air and thereby remains held down by things that have no power to propel her to her Destiny.

You can never go higher than your dreams because it is your dreams that determine how high you go.

To fulfil Destiny, you need to take in all that which is fresh and pure and resist anything stale. Any voice within you speaking of the stale and polluted things you should resist and listen to the voice that speaks of things that are fresh, clean and vibrant.

Whether it be in your family, business enterprise, church ministry, social networks, institution or organization, there will always be voices that seek to pollute you and pull you down and hinder you from fulfilling your Purpose and Destiny (like voices of hatred, gossip, malice, sabotage, underhandedness, corruption, bribery, sexual perversity, unethical dealings etc.). It is important you choose to resist and rise above all these polluted voices and instead listen to the voices that are pure, true and noble.

Destiny Questions To Ponder On

1. *How do you develop a hunger for higher things?*

2. *What hinders you from soaring high?*

3. *What kind of Wells quench you when you are pursuing Destiny?*

4. *What are the mundane things that often erroneously define us?*

5. *How do you yearn for empowerment?*

6. *How do you harness your focus and energy?*

7. *What factors cause you to look down when you really want to look up?*

Chapter Twelve

THE DIARY OF A DESTINY DIVA

Understanding The Kind Of Destiny Woman You Are

Chapter Preview

1. *The Woman who is a "Late Destiny Bloomer"*
2. *The Woman who is a "Destiny Dreamer"*
3. *The Woman who is a "Destiny Chaser"*
4. *The Woman who is a "Destiny Spectator"*
5. *The Woman who is a "Destiny Gypsy"*
6. *The Woman who is a "Destiny Defector"*
7. *The Woman who is a "Destiny Die-Hard"*

OPENING REMARKS

The journey to Destiny has many travellers, each running their own race in their own lane. Each plagued with their own flaws and mixed in their own flavours. Yet each one is a valid sojourner, seasoned and well able to enter their Destiny. It is possible that every Destiny woman will keep her own diary to measure her strides in her journey to Destiny and in the process, she will learn a lot about herself, (especially as regards her strengths and weaknesses). She will discern what tends to propel her and what tends to hold her back.

This Book speaks to different types of women, all seeking to live purposefully and fulfil Destiny, there is the late Destiny Bloomer, the Destiny Dreamer, the Destiny Chaser, the Destiny Gypsy, the Destiny Spectator, the Destiny Defector and the Destiny Die-Hard. Each one will identify with one of these characters and hopefully understand herself better and become more equipped and empowered to fulfil her Destiny.

The use of the word "diva" in this context should be treated with as much tolerance as possible. Even though the women described here are not divas in the true sense of the word, they are nonetheless often misidentified as such by those who fail to understand them. Whether perceived as Divas or not each of these women are serious candidates for Destiny and they should not be dismissed or undermined in any way.

1. THE LATE DESTINY BLOOMER

This is the Woman who writes herself off because she feels that she started her journey to Destiny so late in life. She feels that she has more missed miles than milestones and the distance remaining looks too far and daunting.

"Be not afraid of growing slowly, be afraid of only standing still." ~ **Unknown**

A **Late Destiny Bloomer** is someone who attains or achieves certain things much later in life than her peers due to several factors which may include for example;

A Woman who has a very sheltered life during her teenage and adolescence. Unlike her peers she does not get an opportunity to socialize and understand the lifestyle at that age. By the time she is let out, she finds herself behind schedule in terms of certain social skills like dating, fashion trends and other related issues. She therefore feels awkward among her peers who are well-advanced and she may often give up and retreat.

A Woman who develops late physically in her body so that she becomes the target of cruel jokes. She may lose confidence and develop low self-esteem and a loathing for her body.

A Woman who gets into her career or the job market later than her peers so she finds herself way behind in terms of accomplishing her dreams and goals etc.

"Never worry about the delay of success compared to others because construction of a palace takes more time than an ordinary building." **Unknown**

A Woman who marries later on in her life or gets children when she is much older (way after her peers).

A woman who becomes born again way after her peers. By the time she immerses herself and becomes stable in salvation, she finds herself trying to catch up and get spiritually deep (which may often discourage her and make her feel unworthy). Her ability to discover and fulfil her Calling becomes overwhelming as she feels left behind.

Suffice to say that **Late Destiny Bloomers** often surprise everybody because of their awareness that they are already behind schedule. They therefore make a greater effort to catch up and sometimes they will even overtake those who were ahead of them.

By virtue of being a **Late Destiny Bloomer** and having experienced either discrimination or other disadvantages, a woman will develop a predisposition to be compassionate. Having faced the ups and downs of life she shows greater reflective thinking, a diminished ego-centeredness and a deeper appreciation of the challenges of others.

In addition, because a **Late Destiny Bloomer** will have faced struggles along the way, they are emphatic and very accommodating of others which ultimately causes them to have better leadership skills. They also develop a resilience and a deeper insight as they seek to face the overcoming task of catching up.

At the end of the day, the beauty about a **Late Destiny Bloomer** is that she will often be the most stable and most focused in the journey to Destiny because of her acute awareness that she must never be left behind again.

Notwithstanding, and after reading this series of Books "**The Late Destiny Bloomer**" will blossom and realize that the one who has the greatest impact often takes the longest to be manifested and that it is not how you start but how you finish that matters. She will be encouraged by knowing that the first shall be last and the last shall be first and that delay (no matter how long it may be) is not denial.

2. THE DESTINY DREAMER

This is the woman who is enchanted and captivated with the idea and allure of Destiny. Her every sentence is interjected with the words "my Destiny". Yet no matter how much she dreams and fantasizes; it remains exactly that… a fantasy and a dream. Her dreaming only leaves her frustrated and empty because of an insufficient understanding of what Destiny is and what it entails so that she can turn her dreaming into reality.

"Not all dreamers achieve, but all achievers are dreamers" ~ **Steve Andreas**

The reason that a **Destiny Dreamer** may fail to actualize her dreams could be due to several factors such as fear of failure or fear of success, fear of the responsibility that the actualized dreams will put upon her or procrastination (whereby she is constantly waiting for the perfect timing to actualize her dreams) or just a lack of confidence as to whether her dreams are worth actualizing.

However, if a **Destiny Dreamer** puts her mind to it and decides to make the necessary Destiny choices and decisions then her dreams will begin to manifest and actualize.

"Big dreamers always win." ~ **Unknown**

A **Destiny Dreamer** needs to adopt and embrace the qualities of a real dreamer by writing it down in a language that inspires her and others instead of living in a fantasy world and sleeping on her dreams. Real dreams are strategic so a real dreamer must envision and articulate her dream to become clear and concrete. She needs to be committed because the difference between "could" and "will" is being committed. She must learn to remain tenacious even when things get tough without giving up on her dream. She must be willing to come out of her comfort zone because a real dream will push a real dreamer out of her comfort zone. She must learn to take risks as she steps into the unfamiliar and the unknown. She must be prepared to suffer embarrassment or the risk of failure because a real dreamer should never fear to fail. She should continue to try and try again until her dreams are actualized.

"So many of our dreams, at first seem impossible, then seem improbable, and then when we summon the will, they soon become inevitable." ~ **Christopher Reeve**

She must be able to identify her Destiny helpers and share her dreams with them and be able to receive input and feedback that will make her dreams a reality.

3. THE DESTINY CHASER

The **Destiny Chaser** is one who has moved from dreaming to chasing and she pursues Destiny with everything in her. Yet still, no matter how much she chases it, it remains slippery and illusive because of an insufficient insight as to where it is and in what it is found.

"Go confidently in the direction of your dreams. Live the life you have imagined" ~ **Henry David Thoreau**

Her biggest dilemma is not knowing what she is chasing and how it looks like. She needs to make every effort to understand the principles expounded in this series of books as to how she can discover and lay hold of her unique purpose and what she needs to fulfil it.

"Every great dream begins with a dreamer. Always remember you have within you the strength, the patience and the passion to reach for the stars and to change the world." ~ **Harriet Tubman**

Once a Woman becomes a **Destiny Chaser** she will develop certain characteristics, she will become passionate, her attitude, priorities, desires and interests will align. She will become sacrificial, willing to pay whatever price she needs to pay. She will be willing to fight and overcome all the obstacles in her way. She will embrace tenacity and become consistently optimistic.

"When you stop chasing the wrong things, you give the right things a chance to catch you." ~ **Unknown**

After reading this Series of Books she will hopefully have a radical paradigm shift. Her vision will become more focused as to exactly where to find her purpose and she will finally catch her Destiny with a firm grip.

She will wake up and turn her every Destiny dream into a Destiny action that will turn into Destiny steps that will usher her right to the doorstep of her Destiny reality.

4. THE DESTINY SPECTATOR

This Woman actually knows what Destiny is all about. She is in fact very interested in understanding more and more about Destiny. She attends every seminar and conference, reads every book and listens to every podcast about Destiny, so that she has no excuse as to why she does not embark on fulfilling her own unique Purpose and enter her own Destiny.

"Don't live your life as a spectator, if no one is cheering or booing you, it means that you are not in the game." ~ **Steve Maraboli**

Her decision to be a spectator and her hesitation in participating is probably due to various factors. She may not want the pressure of participating and the expectation of others upon her. She has a lethargy or an inability to give it the seriousness it deserves. It could be a lack of realization as to how meaningless her life is or will be if she continues to side-line her Destiny.

The difference between a spectator and a participant is that a spectator never lays hold of that which others are participating in. To this extent a Destiny spectator will risk not laying hold of her Destiny. She needs to overcome her lethargy, her fear of commitment and responsibility and her comfort zone mentality and agree to step out of the sidelines and participate in the race.

"Life is not a spectator sport. If you are going to spend your whole life in the grandstand just watching what goes on, in my opinion you are wasting your life." **~ Jackie Robinson**

Stop living in the past, get uncomfortable, and learn to handle pressure. However, when this Woman comes to that revelation, she will immerse herself with such a passion and zeal. She will surprise many around her by making great strides in her journey to Destiny than many had expected.

"In life be a participant not a spectator." **~ Lou Holtz**

5. THE DESTINY GYPSY

This is the woman who is already on route but overweight with prohibited baggage and underweight with the mandatory essentials to fulfil Destiny (like trying to board a flight without her passport and ticket but with bags full of fireworks, grenades and other flammables). She has failed to familiarize herself with the "Destiny travel manual".

This Woman needs to critically analyze what she needs and what she does not need in her journey to Destiny (in terms of the tools, relationships, mindset etc.) and offload herself of everything else that is not necessary such as past pain and failures, offences, stale success, wrong mindset etc.

This woman will immerse herself into understanding the "Destiny travel manual" and shed off every weight of baggage that has been slowing her down and take up her empowering luggage and fly towards that which she was created for.

6. THE DESTINY DEFECTOR

This is the woman who feels that the price and the sacrifice of the journey has become all too much. She is no longer convinced that it is worth it. She becomes short sighted in terms of the great impact that finishing her race will have on her generation and future generations.

"You can blame circumstances, but backsliding always begins in the heart." ~ **Aiden Wilson Tozer**

A **Destiny Defector** is basically a backslider and it refers to someone who relapses while in the journey. She therefore loses all the miles she had gained. She either becomes stagnant or at worst she starts going backwards in retrogression. She demonstrates the characteristics of being afraid, of having a blurred vision, an inability to face hardships, inability to be proactive and make prompt decisions, and one who wavers and is double-minded in everything she does.

A **Destiny Defector** is a person who abandons their real cause in favour of an opposing one. When you defect from your Destiny you are basically choosing the opposite of Destiny which is downfall and destruction. It means that you are giving up your allegiance to your Destiny in exchange for an allegiance to your destruction.

This Woman did not grow up saying "when I grow up, I am going to embark in fulfilling my Destiny and then halfway through I will quit". She just needs to surround herself with the right relationships that will edify and encourage her.

"Someone said, backsliding is not a blowout, it's a slow leak." **~ Don Sisk**

This **Destiny Defector** should out her fall and readjust the lens of her mental telescope, so that she stretches her shortsightedness into longsightedness. She will then see the prize awaiting her after she pays the price, and the power that will come from her pain, and the fruit that she will bear from her sacrifice.

She is the woman who feels that she has been in a constant battle zone from the day she resolved to embark on the journey to Destiny. The vicious attacks from her dream and Destiny killers have made her battle fatigued. She convinces herself that she does not have what it takes to defeat those forces. She has an insufficient revelation as to what and how to use that which is already within her to defeat everything that seeks to come against her Destiny.

This woman should make a "Destiny shout" and unleash every weapon that she already has within her and wage a war that will make her the 'Destiny victor' that she was born to be.

7. THE DESTINY DIE-HARD

This is the one who has been one of these other women described here but she comes to a revelation that without laying hold of her Destiny, she will have lived in vain. Over time she has developed a strong reluctance to give up so she vigorously maintains her resolve to fulfil "the what" she was created for and become "the who" she was meant to be.

This Woman therefore remains devoted to her Calling with an extreme and an absolute loyalty to it, willing to make whatever sacrifices she may need to make.

She possesses certain qualities that are guaranteed to propel her to finish her race and finish it well, that spell the word D.E.S.T.I.N.Y

- **Determination** and drive meaning the ability to move with force and focus in the specified direction of her Destiny with an "innate" strong urge to attain and lay hold of it.
- **Effectiveness** and efficiency meaning the ability to accomplish tasks with the least waste of time and effort and the ability to produce the desired results.
- **Self-confidence** meaning a feeling of trust in her abilities, qualities and judgment enabling her to be decisive and proactive and to lay hold of opportunities at a precise moment.
- **Tenacity** meaning the ability to grip and hold on to her goals firmly with persistence no matter how difficult things get.
- **Imagination** meaning, she has the creativity to think and do things out of the box, she is resourceful with an ability to find quick practical solutions in every situation and crisis.
- **Nobility** meaning, she is noble in character, solid in her integrity, full of selflessness, honour, honesty, generosity and bravery
- **Yieldedness** meaning she is submissive willing and able to concede and be flexible and to adjust herself and adapt where wisdom requires her to.

Whether you are a late Destiny bloomer, a Destiny dreamer, a Destiny chaser, a Destiny spectator, a Destiny gypsy, a Destiny defector or a Destiny die-hard, suffice to say you have everything you need within you to fulfil your Destiny irrespective of people's opinions and irrespective of your own initial misgivings as to whether you have what it takes to lay hold of your Destiny.

Destiny Questions to Ponder On

1. *Are you a late Destiny Bloomer?*

2. *Are you a Destiny Dreamer?*

3. *Are you a Destiny Chaser?*

4. *Are you a Destiny Spectator?*

5. *Are you a Destiny Gypsy?*

6. *Are you a Destiny Defector?*

7. *Are you a Destiny Die-Hard?*

This Page Was Intentionally Left Blank

Chapter Thirteen

THE DAILY CONFESSIONS OF A DESTINY CHASER

Reinforcing Your Identity With The Power Of Your Words

Chapter Preview

1. *Confessing the Authority in me*
2. *Confessing the Favour upon me*
3. *Confessing the Wisdom in me*
4. *Confessing my Health and Protection*
5. *Confessing the Strength in me*
6. *Confessing the Provision available to me*
7. *Confessing the Peace in and around me*

OPENING REMARKS

"Align your activity with your Vision. Being consistent and intentional with your daily activity will result in sustainable success." **~ Farshad Asl**

Making daily confessions, decrees and declarations as well as believing them, is crucial as you fulfil your Purpose. Your identity will be attacked and threatened on a daily basis as you face the stresses and pressures of daily life, the poison of people's opinions, as you try to juggle your various roles and as you fight to protect yourself from your vicious dream killers and Destiny destroyers.

Making these daily confessions boldly will affirm you, strengthen you and equip you with the necessary ammunition that you need to face each day.

These daily confessions, decrees and declarations help to set the course of your life with your words and actions that align with your Purpose and Destiny thereby keeping you on track.

Remember that even though you will have Destiny helpers walking this journey with you, there also busy fulfilling their own destinies and ultimately the primary responsibility for your Destiny lies on you, because those Destiny helpers are precisely that, but you are the captain of your Destiny.

Most importantly your confessions should be founded on what you know to be true concerning you and your Destiny.

Confessions, decrees and declarations that are about yourself and your life are closely linked. A confession in this context is a statement settling an essential conviction, an acknowledgement of something you believe to be true about yourself and your life. So, it is crucial that you believe it to be true. A decree in this context is taking a word and speaking it out as a way of enforcing and endorsing it into your life to reiterate what is already true about you and who you are.

A declaration is the act of announcing explicitly facts and truths as a testimony.

These confessions, decrees and declarations have certain fundamental characteristics namely; it has to be spoken out of your mouth even if initially written, that it is a truth with a power to bind and a force to change your reality and set the course of your life.

That is the reason why you must ensure that any personal confession, decree and declaration is positive and beneficial and ultimately aligns you to your Destiny. There is power in your words whether those words be positive or negative.

So, where there are areas in your life that need changing for the better, your tongue is the best tool to use in bringing about that change and transformation. Your tongue is a very powerful instrument that can work for or against you

"Death and life are in the tongue, and those who love it will eat its fruit." **(Proverbs 18:21)**

Your confessions, decrees and declarations can be in relation to the various areas of your life like family, marriage, children, business, career, finances, health, relationships, your dreams and Visions etc.

In addition, they can also be with regard to certain habits and behaviours that you may either wish to form or eradicate from your life by making your daily confessions.

The repetitive nature of your daily confessions is what will embed their truth in to your soul and spirit and ultimately cause you to walk in line with them.

Your daily confessions become pivotal in silencing the negative narratives and negative self-believes in your head about yourself. The mouth speaks what your heart is full of, so once you believe in your heart, then the utterance will flow naturally from your mouth because what you speak is a reflection of your heart.

1. CONFESSING THE AUTHORITY IN ME

Today I CONFESS that I am the head and not the tail, forever above and not beneath.

I have divine insight; I have divine ideas and I have divine authority and I choose to exercise my authority today with my words so that when I decree a thing it shall be so.

Greater is He who is in me than he who is in the world and the same spirit that resurrected Jesus from the dead, lives within me so that I have the power and authority to resurrect things in my life that have died or had been silenced by the enemy.

2. CONFESSING THE FAVOUR UPON ME

Today I CONFESS that I am highly favoured, God's favour surrounds me today as a shield, I expect favour.

Jesus had favour with God and man and as He is so am I on this earth.

Therefore, I shall have favour today with God and man. I expect and receive favour in my home, in my business, in my job, in my ministry, in my finances and in every endeavour I am involved in.

3. CONFESSING THE WISDOM IN ME.

Today **I CONFESS** that I have the wisdom of God, I will think the right thoughts and make the right decisions and choices in every situation I face today. My mouth speaks wisdom and my heart is full of understanding.

I ask for and receive an abundant supply of wisdom and understanding today from God, wisdom from above that is pure, peaceable, gentle, unwavering and willing to yield without hypocrisy.

Wisdom and understanding are better than silver and gold and nothing I desire can compare with them.

I make it my ambition and desire to have understanding and wisdom and therefore I know, I will have all the other desires of my heart.

4. CONFESSING MY HEALTH AND PROTECTION

Today I CONFESS that I have good health and that my words go before me in securing my divine health and healing.

I shall not be sick today and I shall have good health today. I have a covenant with God and by the blood of Jesus I release my divine protection.

I expect divine appointments today, to run in to the right people and to be delivered from the wrong people.

Any adversity attacks, accidents, tragedies that were headed my way are diverted right now in Jesus name.

I stop all attacks, assaults, oppressions and fears from coming to my life.

So, I declare that today I shall not be defeated, discouraged, depressed or disappointed.

5. CONFESSING THE STRENGTH IN ME.

Today I CONFESS that I receive supernatural strength from God and my angels.

I speak to every mountain of fear, every mountain of discouragement, every mountain of stress, every mountain of depression and every mountain of lack and insufficiency and I say, be removed and cast into the sea in Jesus name.

Today I Expect the best day of my life spiritually, mentally, emotionally, relationally and financially in Jesus name.

6. CONFESSING THE PROVISION AVAILABLE TO ME

Today I CONFESS that my steps are ordered by the Lord. I have a covenant with God and by the blood of Jesus, I release my divine provision for today.

I will not be broke today, and I have all the resources I need today in Jesus name.

7. CONFESSING THE PEACE IN AND AROUND ME

Today I CONFESS that I have the peace of God that surpasses all human understanding.

I therefore speak to the raging waters in my life and I say peace be still.

I say to my emotions, my mind, my body, my home and my family peace be still.

I have peace with God, by being aligned to His will in every area of my life.

The above daily confessions are not exhaustive and you may come up with many others regarding any other areas of your life and even concerning your loved ones and others in your circle of concern and influence and even concerning your society, and the various spheres of influence in your nation and other nations that you may have a burden for.

In addition to making these daily confessions it is important to note that how you view yourself, how to present and portray yourself to the rest of the world whether positively or negatively speaks to your ability to be the master and captain of your Destiny.

Before anyone else can see you in a positive light you must be the first one to see and present the "self" in you positively.

It is important that you develop certain self-affirmations that you will make and repeat to yourself as often as possible in order to remain strong and focused in your journey to Destiny.

The Purpose of an affirmation is for self-empowerment, it should be positive not negative and it should be repeated often enough so as to take root. It should be in present tense not past or future tense and it should be personal, specific and clear.

"**Self**" is a person's essential being that distinguishes you from others. Synonymous with your ego, persona, soul, mind and spirit. It is your responsibility to feed the self in you and to keep it positive otherwise the daily stresses and pressures of life as well as the opinions of people will project what is negative in that self.

THE 7 POSITIVE SELFS OF A DESTINY WOMAN

A. WALKING IN SELF-AWARENESS TO AVOID SELF-SABOTAGE

"Self-awareness is a key to self-mastery." ~ **Gretchen Rubin**

Self-awareness is the ability to avoid self-sabotage and self-destruction patterns of behaviour.

Your ability to walk in high emotional intelligence and avoid self-sabotage speaks volumes about who you are.

Self-awareness also speaks to your ability to understand your own emotions and responses and the ability to relate to people and to handle social situations appropriately.

Self-awareness doesn't stop you from making mistakes, it allows you to learn from them. So, it is not the absence of mistakes but your ability to correct them.

Your self-awareness is one of your greatest strengths. You must be emotionally intelligent, to master your emotions, to rule over your thoughts, to guard your heart and tame your tongue, knowing that your real power and authority comes from your self-mastery.

You should be **proactive** instead of reactive

B. WALKING IN SELF-RESPECT TO SAFEGUARD YOUR IDENTITY

Your ability to respect yourself by appreciating your value and relevance contributes greatly to a positive self-esteem and self-worth by ensuring that you do not allow anyone to mishandle, mistreat, misuse, mismanage or undermine you in any way.

It is important to note that self-confidence is not confidence in self because confidence in self implies a negative kind of confidence whereas self-confidence implies a true kind of confidence.

"Low self-esteem is like driving through life with your hand-break on." ~ **Maxwell Maltz**

C. **WALKING IN SELF-CARE TO PRESERVE YOURSELF FOR DESTINY**

You should Purpose to maintain physical, mental and spiritual health and you should Purpose to maintain a balance between my social and work life to avoid burnout.

You should Purpose to practice self–care by taking responsibility for your health (emotionally, mentally and physically) by not overworking or overextending yourself and by running your own race in your own lane without carrying other people's monkeys and failing to say no thereby finding yourself using your energy and time in the wrong things.

Your Self–care also means choosing the right healthy relationships and saying goodbye to unhealthy toxic ones.

You Purpose to walk in self-care to maintain a healthy balance between all areas of your life including your social and work-life to avoid burnout and meltdown.

"Self-care is never a selfish act, it is simply good stewardship of the gift I have, the gift I was put on earth to offer to others." ~ **Parker Palmer**

D. **WALKING IN SELF-GROWTH TO MAXIMIZE YOUR EFFECTIVENESS FOR DESTINY**

Your ability to embrace **self-improvement,** self-growth and to guard your Power of Choice which is the one thing that no one can take away from you, knowing that your ability to respond appropriately in every situation is your responsibility.

You should guard your time jealously, without apology, and discriminate as to who you allow into my space and sanctuary.

You Purpose to take responsibility for my actions, to have a right attitude, to avoid blame shifting, to avoid self-pity and victim syndrome.

You should understand that your ability to take charge over your continued self-improvement and self-development is a sign of a positive self. To self-modify and reinvent yourself when you need to.

E. **WALKING IN SELF-MOTIVATION TO MAINTAIN MOMENTUM TO DESTINY**

To encourage yourself in the Lord when you are distressed, discouraged and disappointed. To avoid over-depending on others but to embrace healthy interdependent relationships.

Your ability to encourage, edify and uplift yourself without relying on others is a positive sign of being healthily self-reliant. While it is good to accept help from others and to be dependent on trusted relationships it is wise to balance your self-dependence with your other dependence so as to strike a healthy balance of interdependence.

F. **WALKING IN SELF-SACRIFICE BECAUSE THERE IS A PRICE TO PAY FOR DESTINY**

You should master self-sacrifice when it comes to giving of your time, gifting, talents, skills and resources for the welfare of others in your circle of love, concern and influence, to be a solution-provider and not a problem creator.

Your responsibility to others in your society and nation and to whom you are assigned. You should know that you are not assigned to everybody or called everywhere so you Purpose to have clarity about your Purpose and place of Purpose to avoid involving yourself with issues that do not fall within your call and mandate.

Your ability to count the cost of what losses you will incur and what it will cost you in fulfilling your Destiny is crucial in determining your ability to self-sacrifice. Equally important is you having a revelation that your journey to Destiny will entail great self-sacrifice and the paying of a high prize, so that you can manage my expectations.

G. **WALKING IN SELF-ANALYSIS TO AVOID SELF-DECEPTION**

You have the ability to regularly and constantly take stock of yourself by self-examination, self-analyses, self- introspection, self-contemplation, soul searching in order to assess where you are emotionally, mentally, physically, intellectually, spiritually as regards your Calling and Purpose so as to be able to take the right action. This entails you taking personal responsibility and accountability.

A daily self-analysis helps you to know where you are at as opposed to where you thought you would be by now.

As we draw towards the end of the year, it is prudent for us as Seasoned Women to do some personal stock taking to appreciate and celebrate our milestones and in the same breath learn from any missed miles as we enter our next season.

In other words, we must ask ourselves "**where am I at?**" **Am I where I thought I would be by now?**

I am reminded of my days at the university in the UK several years ago when some friends and I would take up casual jobs in supermarkets during the spring breaks to make some extra cash (for that very misplaced priority called a Louis Vuitton bag to show off back home in the summer).

During the stock taking in the supermarket, we learnt that the items that were profitable were the ones that sold fast and furiously and they were the ones that needed to be **increased** in the next order, whereas the items that were unprofitable were the slow-moving ones that needed to be **decreased** in the next order.

Likewise in the personal stock taking exercise of our current season, we need to access and **increase** in the acts and habits that were most profitable to us and to **decrease** in the acts and habits that were most unprofitable to us in order to sustain our momentum towards Destiny.

Destiny Questions to Ponder On

1. In which ways do you exercise your divine authority in a daily basis?

2. What does it mean to be favoured, give examples?

3. How do you ensure that you are tapping into God's wisdom every day?

4. How have your daily confessions helped you to overcome challenges in your health and what areas of your life have you experienced God's protection most?

5. What is the difference between having the peace of God, peace with God and peace in God?

6. What is your understanding of provision?

7. What depletes your strength most?

8. What issues in your view cloud your self-awareness most?

9. What steps do you take to ensure that you are constantly walking in self-respect?

10. What dimension in your life do you find you care least for or neglect most, is it your emotions, your mind, your physical, your social etc.?

11. Which area of your life do you believe currently requires the most growth and development?

12. What ways do you employ to self-motivate?

13. In which areas do you feel you have self-sacrificed most in and did you feel it was worth it?

14.How often do you take a self-analysis/self-stock of yourself and how comprehensive is your self-analysis/ self-stock?

WORDS HAVE POWER

Inspirational Quotes and Scriptures About A Woman Of Destiny

Inspirational Quotes and Scriptures about the Woman of Destiny

"Strong women not only feel pain, they accept it, they learn from it and fight through it. They turn their wounds into wisdom. They may fall, but they always get back up, dust off, and fight like they have never fought before." By **Unknown**

"A woman who is at rest with herself has nothing to prove to others, she embraces her strengths & cheers others on with a pure heart. Her light shines brightly; her words are seasoned with kindness, goodness & grace. She is peaceful & edifies others as she is secure in her Heavenly Father." By **Hanna Bryant**

"God has a purpose for your pain, a reason for your struggle and a reward for your faithfulness. Trust Him and don't give." By **Dave Willis**

"She may be quiet, but she's a warrior and her prayers can move mountains." **Unknown**

"She is not broken anymore, she is stronger, wiser and more beautiful than before, because God took her broken pieces and made her new again." By **Unknown**

"Though my soul may set in darkness, it will rise in perfect light; I have loved the stars too fondly to be fearful of the night." By **Sarah Williams**

"In the end, she became more than she was expected. She became the journey, and like all journeys, she did not end, she just simply changed directions and kept going." By **R. M. Drake**

"Mirror! Mirror! on the wall, I'll always get up after I fall. And whether I run, walk or have to crawl, I'll set my goals and achieve them all." By **Brie Edison**

"*I am a strong woman because a strong woman raised me.*" By **Unknown**

"*We all have an unsuspected reserve of strength inside that emerges when life puts us to test.*" By **Isabel Allende**

"*Keep your head up. God gives his hardest battles to his strongest soldiers.*" By **Unknown**

"*If you feel like you are losing everything, remember that trees lose their leaves every year and they still stand tall and wait for better days to come.*" By **Unknown**

"*Strength grows in the moments when you think you can't go on, but you keep going anyway.*" By **Unknown**

"*Some women are lost in the fire. Some women are built from it.*" By **Michelle K**

"*I know you're tired, you're fed up, you're so close to breaking, but there is strength within you even when you feel weak. Keep fighting.* By **Unknown**

"*Strength doesn't come from what you can do. It comes from overcoming the things you once thought you couldn't.* By **Rikki Rogers**

"*It's actually pretty simple. Either you do it, or you don't.*" By **Unknown**

"*She believed she could, so she did.*" By **R.S. Grey**

"*I'm proud of the woman I am because I went through one hell of a time becoming her.*" By **Unknown**

"*The circles of women in our lives weave invisible nets of love that carry us when we are weak, and they sing with us when we are strong.*" By **Sark**

"Behind every successful woman is a tribe of other successful women, who have her back." By **Kimberly**

"Women should empower each other, instead of being so hateful and envious of one another." By **Unknown**

"A successful woman is one who can build a firm foundation with the bricks others have thrown to her." By **Unknown**

"It took me quite a long time to develop a voice, and now that I have it, I am not going to be silent." By **Madeleine Albright**

"She overcomes everything that was meant to destroy her." By **Sylvester McNutt III**

"When women support each other, incredible things happen." By **Viola Davis**

"Each time a woman stands up for herself, she stands up for all women." By **Maya Angelou**

"A woman is unstoppable after she realizes she deserves better." By **Yene D.**

"I am obsessed with seeing women encourage, support, and empower other women. It's my favorite, we need more of it." By **Unknown**

"I would like to be known as an intelligent woman, a courageous woman, a loving woman, a woman who teaches by being." By **Maya Angelou**

"Here's to strong women, may we know them, may we be them, may we raise them." By **Unknown**

"She never seemed shattered; to me she was the breathtaking mosaic of the battles she won." By **Unknown**

"A strong woman, looks a challenge in the eye, and gives it a wink." By **Gina Carey**

"Never underestimate the power of a kind woman. Kindness is a choice that comes from incredible strength." By **Unknown**

"She surrounds herself with women she can grow with." By **Unknown**

"When a woman is loved correctly, she becomes ten times, the woman she was before." By **Unknown**

"A woman unaffected by insult has made her enemies absolutely powerless." By **Entity**

"A strong woman in her essence is a gift to the world." By **Unknown**

"I want every girl to know that her voice can change the world." By **Malala Yousafzai**

"Women who compliment other women genuinely are a whole different breed. Real Queens" By **Unknown**

"Nothing is more impressive than a woman who is secure in the unique way God made her." By **Rhonda Kulczyk**

"Empowered women empower women." By **Unknown**

"A foolish woman keeps talking, a wise woman understands the power of her words as well as her silence." By **Unknown**

"And one day she discovered, that she was fierce, and strong, and full of fire, and that not even she could hold herself back, because her passion burned brighter than her fears." By **Mark Anthony**

"We need women who are so strong, they can be gentle, so educated they can be humble, so fierce they can be compassionate, so passionate they can be rational, and so disciplined they can be free." By **Kavita N. Ramdas**

"A strong woman is a woman determined to do something others are determined not to be done." By **Marge Piercy**

"Be strong enough to let go, and wise enough to wait for what you deserve." By **Unknown**

"Strong women lift each other up." By **Unknown**

"A woman is like a tea bag; you never know how strong it is until it is in hot water." By **Eleanor Roosevelt**

"A strong woman is one, who feels deeply and loves fiercely, her tears flow just as abundantly as her laughter. A strong woman is both soft and powerful, she is both practical and spiritual, a strong woman in her essence is a gift to the world." By **Unknown**

"Strong women wear their pain like stilettos, no matter how much it hurts, all you see is the beauty of it. By **Harriet Morgan**

"Success isn't about how much money you make, it's about the difference you make in people's lives." By **Michelle Obama**

"To attract money, you must focus on wealth. It is impossible, to bring more money into your life, when you are noticing you don't have enough because that means you are thinking thoughts that you don't have enough." By **Rhonda Byrne**

"You can only become truly accomplished at something you love. Don't make money your goal. Instead pursue the things you love doing and then do them so well that people can't take their eyes off you." By **Maya Angelou**

"Here's to financially independent Women, may we know them, may we be them, may we raise them." By **Unknown**

"People, who have drawn wealth into their lives, used the secret consciously or unconsciously, they think thoughts of abundance of

wealth, and they don't allow any contradictory to take roots in their minds." By **Rhonda Byrne**

"Save your money and one day your money will save you." By **Unknown**

"Nearly every glamorous, wealthy, successful career woman, you might envy now, started out as some kind of schlep. By **Helen Gurley Brown**

"A business career for a woman, and her needs for a woman's life, as wife and mother, are not enemies at all, unless we make them so. But maybe the closest and most co-operative friends and supporters of each other." By **Hortense Oldum**

"Leadership is about making others better as a result of your presence and making sure that impact lasts in your absence." By **Sheryl Sandberg**

"Women need to shift from thinking I'm not ready to do that to I'll learn by doing it." By **Sheryl Sandberg**

"If your actions create a legacy that inspires others to dream more, learn more, do more and become more, then, you are an excellent leader." By **Dolly Parton**

"I just want women to always feel in control, because we are capable, we're so capable." By **Nicki Minaj**

"A leader takes people where they want to go. A great leader takes people where they don't necessarily want to go, but ought to be." By **Rosalynn Carter**

"Because I am a woman, I must make unusual effort to succeed. If I fail, no one will say, 'She doesn't have what it takes.' They will say, women don't have what it takes." By **Unknown**

"Our deepest fear is not that we are inadequate. Our deepest fear is that we are powerful beyond measure." By **Marianne Williamson**

"Leadership is hard to define and good leadership even harder. But if you can get people to follow you to the end of the earth, you are a great leader." By **Indra Nooyi**

"People respond well to those that are sure of what they want." By **Anna Wintour**

"No power on earth compares to a mother's tender prayer." By **Edwin Arnold**

"I remember my mother's prayer and they have always followed me. They have clung to me all my life." By **Abraham Lincoln**

"The battle for our children's lives is waged on our knees." By **Stormie Omartian**

"Prayer warrior mothers cover their kids with God's blessings and protection." By **Marla Alupoaicei**

"Every mother's prayer; guide her to a place where she'll be safe." By **Carole Bayer Sager**

"The bond between mothers and their children is one defined by love. As a mother's prayer for her children are unending, so are the wisdom, grace and strength they provide for their children." By **President George W. Bush**

"God does hear and answer prayers. . . From childhood, at my mother's knee where I first learned to pray . . . I know without question that it is possible for men and women to reach out in humility and prayer and tap that Unseen Power." **Ezra Taft Benson**

"During all those years of struggle and heartache, my mother never worried. She took all her troubles to God in prayer." **Dale Carnegie**

"My mother knew when to listen and when to pray and when to help. I wonder how many people knew the compassion [my mother] held for them and how hard, in the privacy of her God Box, she prayed for them and their struggles." **Mary Lou Quinlan**

"To this day, even though I am grown and have two children of my own, whenever I travel somewhere distant or am undertaking a major project, my mother will sit me down, lay hands on me, and say a prayer of blessing." **Francisco J. García** Jr.

"From the time of my earliest memories, she impressed upon me one rule above all others: when I woke from sleep, my first duty was to pray to God for spiritual nourishment and blessings . . . my mother would never relent . . . She planted in me, and tended in my early life, a profound love and fear of God." **Sadhu Sundar Singh**

Bible Wisdom

Proverbs 31:30;"Charm is deceitful and beauty is passing, But a woman who fears the LORD, she shall be praised."

Psalm 46:5 "God is in the midst of her, she shall not be moved; God shall help her, just at the break of dawn."

Proverbs 31:16-17 "She considers a field and buys it; from her profits she plants a vineyard. She girds herself with strength, and strengthens her arms."

1 Corinthians 15:10 "But by the grace of God I am what I am, and His grace toward me was not in vain; but I laboured more abundantly than they all, yet not I, but the grace of God *which was* with me."

Proverbs 31:20-21 "She extends her hand to the poor, Yes, she reaches out her hands to the needy. She is not afraid of snow for her household, For all her household *is* clothed with scarlet."

Psalm 139:14 "I will praise You, for I am fearfully and wonderfully made; Marvellous are Your works, And that my soul knows very well."

1 Corinthians 11:12 "For as woman came from man, even so man also comes through woman; but all things are from God."

1 Peter 3:3-4 "Do not let your adornment be merely outward—arranging the hair, wearing gold, or putting on fine apparel—rather let it be the hidden person of the heart, with the incorruptible beauty of a gentle and quiet spirit, which is very precious in the sight of God."

1 Timothy 3:11 "Likewise, their wives must be reverent, not slanderers, temperate, faithful in all things."

Luke 1:45 "Blessed is she who believed that there will be a fulfilment of those things which were told her from the Lord."

Proverbs.31:20 "She extends her hand to the poor, Yes, she reaches out her hands to the needy."

Proverbs 11:16 "A gracious woman retains honour, But ruthless *men* retain riches."

Proverbs 31:25 "Strength and honour *are* her clothing; She shall rejoice in time to come."

Proverbs 3:15 "She *is* more precious than rubies, And all the things you may desire cannot compare with her."

Proverbs 31:26 "She opens her mouth with wisdom, And on her tongue *is* the law of kindness."

Proverbs. 14:1 "The wise woman builds her house, But the foolish pulls it down with her hands.

Proverbs. 19:13 "A foolish son is the ruin of his father, And the contentions of a wife are a continual dripping."

Proverbs. 21:9 "Better to dwell in a corner of a housetop, Than in a house shared with a contentious woman."

Proverbs. 31: 17–18 "She girds herself with strength, And strengthens her arms. She perceives that her merchandise is good, And her lamp does not go out by night."

Proverbs.21:19 "Better to dwell in the wilderness, Than with a contentious and angry woman."

Proverbs. 31: 16 "She considers a field and buys it; From her profits she plants a vineyard."

Proverbs.12:4 "An excellent wife is the crown of her husband, But she who causes shame is like rottenness in his bones."

Proverbs. 31:19 "She stretches out her hands to the distaff, And her hand holds the spindle.

Proverbs. 31:10-12 "Who can find a virtuous wife? For her worth is far above rubies. The heart of her husband safely trusts her; So, he will have no lack of gain. She does him good and not evil All the days of her life."

Proverbs. 31:13-15 "She seeks wool and flax, And willingly works with her hands. She is like the merchant ships, She brings her food from afar. She also rises while it is yet night, And provides food for her household, And a portion for her maidservants."

Proverbs.31:26 "She opens her mouth with wisdom, And on her tongue is the law of kindness."

Ephesians.5:22-23 "Wives, submit to your own husbands, as to the Lord. For the husband is head of the wife, as also Christ is head of the church; and He is the Savior of the body."

1ˢᵗ Peter. 3:1-2 "Wives, likewise, be submissive to your own husbands, that even if some do not obey the word, they, without a word, may be won by the conduct of their wives, when they observe your chaste conduct accompanied by fear."

Titus. 2:3-5 "The older women likewise, that they be reverent in behaviour, not slanderers, not given to much wine, teachers of good things— that they admonish the young women to love their husbands, to love their children to be discreet, chaste, homemakers, good, obedient to their own husbands, that the word of God may not be blasphemed."

1ˢᵗ Tim. 2:9-10 "In like manner also, that the women adorn themselves in modest apparel, with propriety and moderation, not with braided hair or gold or pearls or costly clothing, but, which is proper for women professing godliness, with good works."

1ˢᵗ Cor. 11:3 "But I want you to know that the head of every man is Christ, the head of woman is man, and the head of Christ is God."

1ˢᵗ Tim.5:14 "Therefore I desire that the younger widows marry, bear children, manage the house, give no opportunity to the adversary to speak reproachfully."

Col.3:18-19 "Wives, submit to your own husbands, as is fitting in the Lord. Husbands, love your wives and do not be bitter toward them."

Proverbs.31:27 "She watches over the ways of her household, And does not eat the bread of idleness."

2ⁿᵈ Tim.1:5 "when I call to remembrance the genuine faith that is in you, which dwelt first in your grandmother Lois and your mother Eunice, and I am persuaded is in you also."

Proverbs.31:28 "Her children rise up and call her blessed; Her husband also, and he praises her."

Proverbs.31:25 "Strength and honour are her clothing; She shall rejoice in time to come."

Proverbs 18:22 "He who finds a wife finds a good thing, And obtains favour from the LORD."

Proverbs.23:22 "Listen to your father who begot you, And do not despise your mother when she is old."

Proverbs.4:6 "Do not forsake her, and she will preserve you; Love her, and she will keep you."

Proverbs.11:22 "As a ring of gold in a swine's snout, So is a lovely woman who lacks discretion."

Proverbs.31:21 "She is not afraid of snow for her household, For all her household is clothed with scarlet."

BIBLIOGRAPHY

The Bible

Jakes, T.D. 2002. *God's Leading Lady: Out of the Shadows and into the Light*. Berkley.

Sandberg, Sheryl & Scovell, Nell. 2013. *Lean In: Women, Work, and the Will to Lead*. Alfred A. Knopf.

Stigel, V. Herta. 2011. *The Mountain Within: Leadership Lessons and Inspiration for Your Climb to the Top*. McGraw-Hill Eductaion.

Scott, Janny. 2011. *A Singular Woman: The Untold Story of Barack Obama's Mother*. Riverhead Books.

Meyer, Joyce. 2010. *Eat the Cookie… Buy the Shoes: Giving Yourself Permission to Lighten Up*. FaithWords.

Karssen, Gien. 1974. *Her Name is Woman*. NavPress Publishing Group.

Live By Faith by Rev. Teresa Wairimu

Yancey, Philip. 2002. *Where Is God When It Hurts?* Zondervan.

Shellenberger, Susie & Gowler, Kathy. 2007. *What Your Daughter Isn't Telling You: Expert Insight Into the World of Teen Girls.* Bethany House Publishers.

Boundaries by Pastor Sammy Hinn

Covey, R. Stephen. 2004. *The 7 Habits of Highly Effective People: Powerful Lessons in Personal Change.* Free Press.

Dr. D. W. Ekstrand, 2012. The Influence Parents have on their Children. Accessed on 28th July, 2020 http://www.thetransformedsoul.com/additional-studies

Sasha, 2016: The influence of a good teacher can never be erased. Accessed on 28th July, 2020 https://mirrorgirlblog.wordpress.com/2016/09/17/

Leslie Becker-Phelps, PHD, 2005; Ways your Friends Influence your Future. Accessed on https://blogs.webmd.com/relationships/20160928

Brandon Thomas, 2008: Does past experience affect what we see or what we do? accessed on 29th July, 2020 https://www.researchgate.net/post/Does_past_experience

Art Markman, Ph.D. 2011: Your View of the Future Is Shaped by the Past. Accessed on 29th July, 2020 https://www.psychologytoday.com/us/blog/ulterior-motives/201108

Orit E. Tykocinski and Andreas Ortmann. 2011: The Lingering Effects of Our Past Experiences: The Sunk-Cost Fallacy and the Inaction-Inertia Effect. Accessed on 29th July, 2020 http://portal.idc.ac.il/he/schools/psychology/

Claire Newton. 2020: Destiny: Action or Accident? Accessed on 29th July 2020 http://www.clairenewton.co.za/my-articles/destiny-action-or-accident.html

Sandra Dawes. 2014. Following your inner voice. Accessed on 29th July, 2020 https://embraceurdestiny.com/2014/01/29/following-your-inner-voice/

Kenneth Copeland, 2018. Ways to Know If You're Hearing God's Voice. Accessed on 29th July, 2020 https://blog.kcm.org/4-ways-know-youre-hearing-gods-voice/

Pincott Jena E, 2019. Silencing Your Inner Critic, accessed on 29th July, 2020 https://www.psychologytoday.com/us/articles/201903/silencing-your-inner-critic

Bonnie Badenoch, Ph.D. 2010. Critical Inner Voice. Accessed on 29th July, 2020 https://www.psychalive.org/critical-inner-voice/